Published by The FAR Press

An imprint of Blaise Publications

Cleveland, Ohio

www.thefarpress.com

Printed in the United States of America

Library of Congress Cataloging-in-Publication-Data

Name: LaGuardia, Joseph author.

Title: Biblical Joe

Description: Cleveland: The FAR Press [2017]

Identifiers: LCCN 2018937658 | ISBN 9780998967530

Praise for Biblical Joe

"Biblical Joe is a book of golden nuggets. Here the author discloses insights from Scripture and life experiences that cause us to wonder, ponder, celebrate and give thanks. If you are tired of the everyday humdrum of life, then you will love this book because it speaks to us of the heart's restless longing for goodness, beauty and truth, as these gifts are unwrapped by the one who seeks God."

Ilia Delio, OSF, Villanova University

"Through poetry, sermon, and prayer, Joe LaGuardia leads us on a beautiful journey sharing his vision for a life grounded in love and intertwined with God. He presents us with a transformational spirituality that re-envisions our opportunities to experience intimacy while engaging the divine. His words will touch your heart and lead you on a path to new sacred possibilities."

Richard Rohr, OFM, Author of Falling Upward

"The words of Joe LaGuardia's poems are creative. They create images that evoke sensory experiences for the reader. Vicariously, our senses of taste, touch, smell, hearing, and sight come alive as we read and imagine, ponder and reflect. In Joe's poems, one is refreshed and nourished to continue one's journey of life."

George Matejka, Ph.D. Professor of Philosophy at Ursuline College

"In this book, LaGuardia offers a voyage through a joyful and revolutionary spirituality. In doing so, he calls us to recognize in ourselves what it means to be human."

Xochitl Alvizo, Ph.D., California State University at Northridge and Co-Editor of Women Religion Revolution

"LaGuardia's theological reflections are life-giving and remind us that the divine is everpresent in our world. A brilliant read with tones of comfort and love."

Jennifer Zobair, Author of Painted Hands

Biblical Joe

Reflections on Life

Biblical Joe

Reflections on Life

Joseph R. LaGuardia

fp

Contents

Foreword   i

Reflections   17

Jeremiah & Ezekiel   19

Canticle of Canticles & Isaiah   21

Proverbs & Ecclesiastes   23

Comments on the Psalms   25

Luke 17:5-10   27

Another Look at Lepers   31

Conflict Old and New   35

From Rape to Murder:
1 Kings 18:17-40   39

Let Me Help You?John 13:5-17   43

Are You Chosen? Am I?   45

Infancy Narratives   47

Laborers in the Vineyard:
a Difficult Passage?   49

"You Have Heard That It Was Said, But I Say…" 55

Passages That I Hate 59

Women Should Be Silent! 61

Noah in the Movies 65

Subduing and Dominating 69

The Rich Young Man &
Redistribution of Wealth 73

A Communion Meditation
In February 77

A Communion Meditation 79

It Is Finished–Good Friday 2015 81

Poetry 87

Cameo 89

God Must Be Like That 90

Micah's Daughter 91

On a Minister's Leaving 93

These Four 94

You Have Been a Light (1 John 1:7) 95

Of Immense Significance–
First Floor Men's Room   97

The Search   98

Why? A Christmas Poem 2013   99

Flirting God   101

Prayers   103

Numbering Our Days Alright   105

Prayer for Worship   106

Autumn Prayer   107

On the Edge of Autumn   108

Snowflake Prayer   109

Spring Prayer 2014   110

We Showed Up   111

New Beginnings Prayer
after Genesis 1-3   112

Pastoral Prayer 11-6-16   113

Pastoral Prayer   115

Sermons   117

   No Charge for Baggage   119

   When the Door Is Barred   127

   Stranded   135

   From Winter to Spring 2015   139

   Substitution   147

   Archaeology   151

   Selling Jesus on EBay   159

   Religion and Politics   165

   A Different Format   173

Foreword

by Gina Messina

Although he often referred to himself as a "nobody," Joseph LaGuardia is a person who touched countless lives and made our world a more loving place.

Joe was the first person to welcome me to Ursuline College in 2013. Before I began my position as dean, Joe, who was serving as interim dean, met with me every week for about 2 months. As we both transitioned to new roles, we exchanged gifts without knowing the other had purchased one. We laughed that we both bought each other books. Joe shared with me his book of poetry *Life Seasons*, a brilliant and touching read. And I gave Joe the book *The Presidents' Club* and joked with him that as only those who had served as presidents knew what it was like in the oval office, he and I were in the Dean's Club, and we were among the few who knew what it was like to serve in the dean's office.

I was so fortunate that Joe agreed to continue to mentor me and we met weekly for breakfast, lunch, etc. to discuss how to manage the many things that would pop up in the world of academic administration. It was not long before Joe and I became very close friends.

Joe knew that I identify as a feminist. He told me that it was clear the College wanted to grow in a new direction based on my hiring, and also warned that there were many who were not comfortable with the idea of a feminist in a leadership position at our Catholic women's college. While Joe was completely comfortable with it, he was clear that feminism was not a part of his identity.

Thus, our many conversations about academic leadership also grew to include feminist and theological thought – as Joe was a theologian himself. Soon, Joe began reading feminist theological content. He quickly took to Rachel Held Evans and Sarah Besse and subscribed to both of their blogs. Every day he would share with me what he had read from both of these women, as well as the latest from FeminismandReligion.com. Shortly thereafter, Joe acknowledged that he had discovered that indeed he is a feminist – although I had known it all along.

Joe's favorite feminist work is *Longing for Running Water* by Ivone Gebara. I loaned him my copy and he apologetically returned a brand new book because the pages were so worn from him reading and re-reading her words that had touched his heart and influenced his thoughts. I insisted that he keep the fresh copy – I wanted the worn copy to remind me of how much he appreciated Gebara's wisdom.

I called Joe my BFF, a title he cherished. Every birthday and Christmas, Joe always surprised me with a thoughtful gift – something that proved he knew me so well – and would sign the card, "your BFF."

Our colleagues recognized the close bond between us. Our friendship crossed gender and generations and I like to believe that we learned from each other. However, the truth is, Joe gave so much of himself to everyone, his spirit and love know no bounds. It is I who has been given such a gift by knowing Joe. He taught me what the beauty of our lives is all about.

Joe is not only my mentor and friend. He is family. In fact, my family knows Joe and his wife Bernadette well, and my daughter Sarah adores them. Joe often brought coloring books for Sarah and would sit and draw with her when she was with me.

The same can be said about Ursuline College. Joe loved Ursuline and all of his colleagues. No matter what was going on, he made sure to attend because it was important to him to show his support to each of the members of the Ursuline Community. For Joe, serving as dean was a highlight in his career. But what he did not realize is that it was also a highlight for every faculty member that served in his school. He always focused on uplifting the faculty sharing with them their strengths and the gifts he saw them bringing to Ursuline.

When Joe decided to retire, it was a difficult and frightening time for him. He feared leaving Ursuline would disconnect him from so many people he cared deeply for – and also feared he would have nothing to do. I can't help but laugh when I think of these conversations. No one ever forgot Joe and he continued to see his colleagues at the many events he would attend. And, I think he was busier in retirement than when he was a full-time dean.

Although nothing made Joe happier than to sit in solitude, write, and read, and focus on spiritual growth, he selflessly always gave his time to others. Joe led bible study and was a member of his church choir. He continually helped members of his church community by driving them to doctors appointments, helping with moving, and so much more. He participated in caring for the church community garden and also gave sermons quite frequently. In fact, he was scheduled to give a sermon the day after he passed on the topic of sanctuary – he was so looking forward to it.

Joe adored his wife, Bernadette, children, Jeannine and Jonathan, and his grandchildren, Eloise and "Cranky Frankie." He loved being the proud grandpa showing pictures of his grandchildren and the wonderful things they were doing. He also loved his cabin in Tidioute, PA. He and Bernadette would go there nearly every weekend during the summer and often with his children and grandchildren. He called it "a little slice of heaven." It is fitting that his ashes are spread there.

Joe also loved Cleveland sports – but no team more than the Tribe – although he swore never to don a hat or any other article of clothing that imaged Chief WaHoo. Attending games with his brother David was a joy for him. When he talked about it he was like a schoolboy who had been to a baseball game for the first time.

Joe and I had lunch Wednesday, October 11th – as we did nearly every week for more than four years – and we had a deep conversation about God. Joe said he struggled with some interpretations of God and wanted to believe that God loved him no matter his sins. I told Joe that God put him on this earth to be an example to the rest of us – and I truly believe that.

While Joe often referred to himself as a "nobody," in fact, Joe was somebody who changed the path of so many lives through his gracious compassion and love. I have no doubt our world is a better place because of the life of Joseph LaGuardia – not the airport or the mayor – but the teacher who taught so many what it means to be a human being.

As a prolific writer, Joe honored many through his craft and kept a blog called BiblicalJoe.com. This book is a compilation of those writings and a tribute to his life's work. Joe always had the perfect words in every situation and that is so well demonstrated in this volume. Here you will find reflections, poetry, prayers, and sermons that will allow you to delve into a transformational spiritual journey that reminds us that God is love and that we are called to reflect such love in our daily lives and recognize it in every perfect detail that surrounds us.

I had the privilege of attending a sermon that Joe gave at his church shortly after I began at Ursuline. It is called "A Different Format" and can be read in the final chapter of this volume. I still remember clearly that he spoke of the book *Proof of Heaven*. He talked about his wife looking for an audiobook to return to the library and a few days later she realized it was an audio file rather than a CD. Joe said that is how we should understand our lives. He said we never die, instead, we are always evolving and changing formats through space and time. I believe that. And I know when Joe met God on Saturday morning, October 14th, 2017, that God welcomed him, embraced him with love, and said, "well done, good and faithful servant" (Matthew 25:21).

Reflections

Jeremiah & Ezekiel

Rev. Richard Rohr, in his daily meditations for April 29 and 30, 2012, writes about the world, the flesh and the devil as sources of violence in our contemporary society as they were in all of past history.[1] In dealing with the world, Father Rohr reminds us that this one is the most invisible. We are almost entirely focused on the flesh and individual "sin."

It is much more difficult to see the evil in our culture and our establishments and our systems. This is what the prophets were good at, and probably why they are and were mostly ignored. Jeremiah hated this role. He knew God chose him for it, but that didn't keep him from disliking what he had to say and do. Everyone considered him unpatriotic because he was calling into question what the society at that time felt was the only way to speak and act.

An article on global warming and "The Climate Fixers" by Michael Specter in the May 14 issue of *The New Yorker* reminds us of the relevance of these two prophets.[2] Depending on which political party you follow, the effects of CO_2 emissions on the planet are either to be dismissed or are dire prophecies of the end of the world as we know it. Still, Specter introduces several people and organizations that are working on solutions to global warming, and offer some reason for hope.

And both Jeremiah and Ezekiel offer hope– Ezekiel in his famous passage concerning the dry bones. Believers throughout the ages have placed their hope in the Lord, and have put this hope against all the doomsayers of every age.

However, that does not mean that we do nothing, and simply let causes of global warming go unchallenged. In our American culture which is based on capitalism, it may be the religious people who have to call attention to the evils that capitalism can allow, and be the people who say NO, even when profits and shareholders and boards do not

1   Richard Rohr. "Daily Meditations." Retrieved from https://cac.org/category/daily-meditations/.

2   Michael Specter. "The Climate Fixers." The New Yorker, 14 May 2012.

permit corporations to control their emissions nor their seeking for greater income.

Canticle of Canticles & Isaiah

Barbara Brown Taylor, in her book *An Altar in the World*, encourages practices of prayer and meditation that are NOT abstract and in some ideal place, but are feeling the dirt between your toes and hearing the birds sing and relishing every gritty detail about being on this earth.

Eckhart Tolle' in *The Power of Now*, encourages meditation that goes into the body. He advises such techniques as listening to the silence between sounds, or following the sound of a bell into silence, or following your breathing into the body. The idea, of course, is to quiet the mind and the ego so that there is space for the present, the now, and the divine.

The Canticle of Canticle is a perfect book for getting into the body. There is a whole history of interpretations of this book, from the first time it was acknowledged as part of Scripture. Interpreters were quick to create an allegorical and a mystical interpretation, to get away from its flagrant eroticism and so to interpret it as a dialogue between God and Israel or between Christ and the Church. After all, there is a biblical history of understanding God's relationship with humans as similar to the relationship between a bride and a bridegroom. –Because, whenever we say 'love,' we are raising implications of romantic, physical love.

Taylor has a shocking passage about this.[1] She relates a conversation with a fellow minister about attraction and spiritual intimacy with God. The union with God is very, very similar on our human level to that between a husband and wife, with that idealized sexual love in this marvelous book called the Canticle of Canticles.

It may be a relief to turn the page from the Canticle and arrive in the Bible at the Prophet Isaiah, except that he, too, acknowledges our fleshly humanness, even in writing these lines which Christians have long understood as referring to Jesus and his Mother: "...the virgin

1   Barbara Brown Taylor. *An Altar in the World*. (New York: Harper Collins, 2009) 38.

shall be with child, and bear a son, and shall name him Immanuel" (7:14).   Sex is how we continue to live, to populate the world, and to experience one of the greatest pleasures and closeness this world has to offer. Isaiah could be considered implying that it is the way the divine enters the world.

The mystics, the enlightened contemplatives, acknowledged this and were able to integrate it into their spirituality. They could look at a picture of St. Teresa of Avila in ecstasy and understand the physicality of it without being thrown. They had come to a place where the physical and the divine were no longer opposites. They could imagine God as spouse, lover, embracing, kissing and becoming one. They could hold us, as Isaiah did, to the necessity of seeking, holding, and loving God.

Proverbs & Ecclesiastes

These two books offer many temptations: for example, to discuss the pros and cons of spanking as a form of discipline; or to expound on the dangers of taking every word of Scripture literally as if it were addressed to us in 2012 directly by God; or to take Proverbs at least as a rule book, as if we were a CPA and got the tax book dumped in our laps with the injunction: "Learn this and you won't be penalized."

Some cultures have a lot of proverbs. German is certainly one of them. I still remember a few, such as "Arbeit macht das Leben suess" ("Work makes life sweet") which comes perilously close to the saying over Auschwitz in Poland and other concentration camps: "Arbeit macht frei" ("Work makes one free"). Surely the placing of this proverb is an example of how a positive sounding sentence can be converted into something ideologically and morally perverse.

Can you live your life by proverbs? What can you do with a proverb such as "The early bird catches the worm?" It surely states a truth that can be used to educate, say, a young person who insists on sleeping in every morning and coming late to school?

The structure of the book of Proverbs seems to indicate that their purpose WAS education, either as passages of instruction or as one or two-line statements. A father is addressing a child; an elder a young initiate. The book fits right in with Rev. Richard Rohr's contemporary writings on the first half and the second half of life.

In the first half of life, we all need rules and discipline. Without training and structure, the rest of our life is a mess. We have no foundation to stand on, to jump from. In the second half of life, we have less need of rules. Hopefully, we can come to some of the wisdom we read about in these two books of the Bible.

One question educators ask is whether wisdom is transferable. Information can be passed on; facts learned; skills acquired. But wisdom? Can quoting a proverb to someone have a positive effect? Or do we have to have the experience to lead us to say when we hear a proverb: Yes! That's right! I know that to be true. But surely there's no harm in trying one out—to try getting up early to see if the old proverb is true for us, or whether another hour of sleep makes us much more efficient.

Generations and generations have believed in passing along wisdom and virtue to the young. The old McGuffey Readers were full of stories with a moral. The morality plays were the same, and when novels were first written, people were scandalized when the good guys didn't win. Some of us would like to find a way back to that culture—when values seemed shared by the majority and bad behavior was uniformly condemned instead of justified by a kind of unstated proverb: If everyone does it, it must be okay. Or: it's okay if you don't get caught.

The Hebrew Bible is certainly not valueless. The stories make it clear that there are consequences for actions and that bad behavior does not go unpunished.

But all of this can't distract us from Jesus' message in these Sundays after Easter: God loves us. He knows we're not perfect. He gives the same wages to those who start late. He is the paradigm of one who knows how to forgive. And He ends up being our true Wisdom!

Comments on the Psalms

It is fitting that after Lent and Easter, we allow ourselves to attend the concert of songs which are the Psalms. We read the story of the Passion of Jesus from Mark's Gospel this year, and echoes of Psalm 22 rang in our ears when the soldiers divided his garments and especially when Jesus began to pray the first verse of this psalm in his agony: "My God, my God, why have you forsaken me?" This verse has come to be known as the "Fourth Word" from the Cross, although for Mark and Matthew it is the ONLY word.

John has references to Psalms 69 and 34 in his account of the Passion, both referring to thirst.

These references confirm Tim Beal's point that "The Psalms give voice to the tremendous depth and breadth of human experience..."[1] The Alleluias of Easter are there, too, and great hope, confidence and joy. If we were to "sing to the Lord a new song" every day, some people would use the psalms, picking one that matches their life situation, their need, their fear, or their heart's being full of thanksgiving and joy.

The psalms have not lost their popularity. Although some books of the bible are read and preached about infrequently, something of the Psalms usually finds its way into worship every Sunday. When the Cleveland Ecumenical Institute scheduled a four week course on the Psalms taught by Rabbi Roger Klein, forty people signed up, and we had to close the enrollment because of lack of space! A priest came to hear the Jewish interpretation of the Psalms. Rabbi Klein brought with him the original Hebrew text, intending to use the original language at times to enlighten the understanding of the translation.

Beal chooses just 6 psalms to include in his book on *Biblical Literacy*. They are good choices. What mood do they evoke? In 1926, Archibald MacLeish wrote a poem about the nature of poetry, and concluded it with a line that used to be famous: "A poem should not

---

1   Tim Beal. *Biblical Literacy*. (New York: Harper One, 2010) 144.

mean, but be!" It was a modernist statement, wanting poems to be like little gems which we could hold up to the light and see the intricacy and ingenuity of their structures as if we were seeing all the colors of the rainbow, dazzling us with their beauty.

That MacLeish quote, however, doesn't seem to apply to the Psalms at all, and never has. As Beal points out, they do have intriguing parallel structures, and contain lots of imagery, symbols and analogies. But they are not read for their beauty. Many people might comment on the beauty of a Psalm 23, perhaps the most popular among the 150 songs, but people who know that psalm have held on to its verses with their fingernails when their lives seemed destined to drown in the shadows of this life's darkest valleys.

The Resurrection convinces believers that we can get THROUGH those dark times, and come out with a "new song" on our lips, perhaps that from Psalm 149: "Sing to the Lord a new song of praise...For the Lord loves his people/and he adorns the lowly with victory...Alleluia."

Luke 17:5-10

There are many "difficult passages" in the Bible. By difficult passages, I mean those that:

> 1. Are difficult to understand. Some of Jesus' parables and sayings will fall into this category;
>
> 2. Seem to require us to do the impossible—the story of the rich young man leaps to mind;
>
> 3. Contradict other passages, such as this week's passage from Luke 17;
>
> 4. Portray a harsh, punitive, vengeful image of God or Jesus—think of some of those Old Testament passages;
>
> 5. Belong to a culture and an era long vanished and so are VERY difficult to apply to our contemporary lives.

Well, there may be more. Dealing with difficult passages is fraught with peril, because we may end up studying them and discussing them and be no further in understanding at the end of our study than we were at the beginning. We may be forced to just give up and say: "Yup! That surely is a difficult passage!"

The other peril is treating these passages just as some fundamentalists treat "proof passages"–find passages that suit your world outlook, political persuasion, or religious point of view and lift them out of context to swing them like weapons to swat down non-believers or puff up those who hold the same points of view. We'll have to be careful about context.

Indeed, some preachers are afraid of the "lectionary" which sets reading for each Sunday and holiday of the liturgical year because these readings put the preacher into unfamiliar territory or challenge him or her to squeeze precious drops of moral persuasion from words that seem cold as stone or even forgiving of practices the preachers would like to rail against [carrying out the punishments of the Law would be one example].

But then we have people like Karen Armstrong who encourage us to wrestle with Biblical passages as Jacob wrestled with an Angel in the Book of Genesis, until we discover compassion in them, which is another way of saying: "until we discover God in them." And remember Walter Brueggemann's talk at Trinity Wall Street,[1] who asks: can the Bible provide us with a place to stand amid the reductionism of science, the capricious hunger and injustice of much of the world, the failure of the nation-states, and the poverty of scientific solutions? He wants us to allow the text to be generative, not static. Forgive this long passage from the notes I took during his talk, but I think there are items of importance here as we begin our trek through difficult passages:

> 1. E.g. meditate on hesed in Psalms 103 and 109. No one quotes Psalm 109, but it gives us four uses of hesed that come from a negative review of it. We get a different idea of steadfast love and reliability. But one doesn't ask who said these words and when or if the events they refer to really happened. They generate new worlds for us.

> 2. Social/scientific and political criticism. See how the text is embedded in power relationships. See the liberal, the feminist, the post-colonial interpretations. To use this ideology gives us a mode of self-discovery: that I am more in the fray than I am aware of. I am interpreting out of my own convictions. We occupy a field of power, we have vested stakes. The texts are full of advocacy for a certain perspective. We are like the scribes, the priests; we come from an economic situation; we have been greatly influenced by our teachers.

> 3. Therefore, we cannot imagine that our claims are objective. The more people we let into the room, what we thought was objective can now be seen as advocacy on our part. See what

---

1   Walter Brueggemann. "Reading Scripture Through Other Eyes.:" Trinity Wall Street, Columbus, Ohio. January 16, 2011.

the advocacies are in the text, what the disputes are. Are they desirable, resisted? Arrive at new dialogic exchange that may lead to transformation. *THERE IS NO DISINTERESTED IN-TERPRETATION!*

4. Copy Jewish modes of interpretation of scripture that do not more quickly to closure. The Rabbi tells you a story and then another story to explain that one. Again, Freud teaches us: we walk around a memory, a dream, an event, a phrase. Each of these has an endless capacity for multiple meanings and can bring great insight. The self is thick (=freighted with more complex meaning), layered (through repression of hurts, rage, and joys), and conflicted (between the felt self and the socially accepted self).

5. Therefore, the scriptural texts are also thick (always more there; we preach on the same one over and over), layered (e.g. JEDP), and conflicted (therefore, these conflicts should not be covered over or screened out by the lectionary).

6. The post-critical person loves these levels, approaches them with wonderment and silence and awe and utterance and re-fused "thinness."

7. We can say the same of God in the text: He is thick, layered and conflicted.

So this sets some background and lights up a path in the dark that we may want to take into this approach to scripture. As Richard Rohr writes in in his book of meditations, entitled *Yes, And*:

The Bible is actually a conflict book. It is filled with seeming con-tradictions or paradoxes, and if you read it honestly and humbly it should actually create problems for you

The way you struggle with the fragmentation of the Bible is the way you probably struggle with your own fragmentation and the fragmen-tations of everything else. The Bible offers you a mirror that reflects back to you how you live life in general. There are very high levels of consciousness and holiness in the biblical text, and texts which are frankly hateful, selfish, and punitive. You need to recognize them as such.[2]

So let's gingerly approach or dive right in (your choice) to this passage from Luke 17:5-10.   I chose it after I read Rachel Held Evans's reflection, "Make it Work."[3]

The difficulties she finds are the Disciples' request that Jesus increase their faith, and what that might mean in the light of his reply, which doesn't seem to make sense, since why would anyone want to throw a mulberry bush into the ocean?   And then there's the difficult example Jesus uses about the servant and his master.   In other passages, Jesus seems to want to upend that vertical social structure.   Rachel has answers; she has a point of view.   Her answers make us think.   They are generative, don't you think?

2   Richard Rohr. *Yes, And...Daily Meditations*. (Cincinnati, Ohio: Franciscan Media, 2013) 28.

3   Rachel Held Evans. "Make it Work": A Homily on Luke 17: 5-10." October 9, 2013. Retreived from https://rachelheldevans.com/blog/make-it-work-homily-luke-17?rq=Luke%20.

Another Look at Lepers

In previous reflection, we did NOT focus on the story of the ten lepers that was the lectionary's choice, but chose instead the verses in Luke 17 that came just before it (17:5-10).

However, there is no denying that the lepers' story is or can be a difficult passage in scripture. Like the earlier verses, it's about faith ("Your faith has healed you," Jesus says to the Samaritan who returned to say thank you). I love the idea presented by Cam Miller that the Samaritan was ALREADY unclean, and whether he was cleansed of leprosy or not, the temple clergy would still have had nothing to do with him. He couldn't show himself to a temple priest. He might as well have gone home.

The Samaritan's predicament adds a new flavor to Jesus's comment about his faith. The Samaritan did not show himself to a priest. Instead, he came back to the Jewish teacher (Rabbi) who healed him and acknowledged what a miracle had occurred in his life and how grateful he was.

It makes me wonder if the nine others were caught up in their prescribed rituals and saw no NEED for faith. They noticed their disease was gone and knew the drill–they had to get to a priest to verify this cure so that they could resume their lives. I wonder if they took things for granted: You get leprosy, it gets healed, you get it verified, that's all there is.

But besides taking a backwards look at the lepers' story, last week we noticed the first four lines of this chapter contain some VERY strong words from Jesus, words that could be used to justify capital punishment, I think. It's a small step, is it not, to actually tie the equivalent of a millstone around the neck of a child abuser or child pornography addict rather than just agree it would be better if…

How strange that this draconian statement should be followed by language of forgiveness–as many times as it takes. Do you suppose such words give hope to those enmeshed in those vices?

Of course, the catch is that word 'repent.'   –Not a free pass to continue nefarious behavior. And so we get to the serious problem of all sinners and addicts: They may feel terrible about their thoughts and actions, but they don't want to give them up. It's like hating your foul habit of smoking, but not taking the steps necessary to break the addiction to nicotine.

So where does that leave us? Do only the pure, the reformed and the brave get into the kingdom? Or is it time to remember the lady with the lost coin and the shepherd with the one sheep gone astray? Those are also in Luke's Gospel (chapter 15). The spirit is at work. Someone is seeking, chasing, not giving up. There was a news report in The Cleveland Plain Dealer about a priest arrested for soliciting sex.

He has lost everything. He already has contracted a life-threatening disease. He has become a leper. Who can even support him without appearing to condone his actions? Because of the demands of his religion and his status, he could not have chosen to be an openly gay man, seeking and dating a partner for the possibility of a loving, enduring and faithful relationship. Could that have prevented this awful descent into darkness and shame?

What must his prayer be like? How many times has he already repented? What can faith mean for him but a dogged hanging on to a God who could cure lepers, Samaritans or not, grateful or not?

I've seen what happens when a person who has been at death's door, is healed by good medical care, and comes back to the applause and hugs of his friends. It reduces everyone to mush, to an overwhelming sense of gratitude. So what would be the experience of having faith that the God who sees everything about you, looks past all the addictions and sins and corruption and opens his/her arms to embrace and kiss away the wounds?

Would we chide and attempt to rebuke such a God? Would we

want to stop worshipping a God who seems to condone evil and forgives criminals?

Jesus didn't seem to demand conditions–not even faith– from those lepers before he cured them. But he praised it when he saw it, especially in that one stranger whom everyone of his race hated.

Conflict Old and New

As last week's lectionary passage from Luke resonates in our memories, I cannot resist citing Cam Miller's sermon, "The Physics of Pain or Gallstones of the Soul."[1]

His sermon calls us to look into conflicts that we avoid above all costs —even people that we avoid—as the judge does in the story of the widow seeking justice in Luke 18. His sermon also challenges us to struggle with God, just like Jacob did on the night his name was changed to Israel (in Genesis 32).

Dealing with and discussing these issues may also help us resolve that very difficult passage that is only one chapter away from the Jacob wrestling match—the story of the rape of Dinah in Chapter 34. Dinah's rape and the terrible revenge for it that Jacob's sons took forces us to consider the position of women in that age and in ours.

It is so difficult to imagine ourselves in another culture, in an age when women were protected by their husbands, brothers, fathers but no one else, and could be traded for money, land, and power. In the Genesis story, we moderns get the distinct impression that the rape was avenged not so much for Dinah's honor as for the tribe of Israel's honor. The Israelites were offered assimilation by the Canaanites—what's ours is yours, even our own wives and daughters—and they were having none of it.

Trust was surely an issue, of course, when it comes to cultures merging in such a way, and the narrator of this chapter in Genesis reveals in the story that something devious was happening as the Canaanites made their 'generous' offer to the Israelites: "Will not their livestock, their property, and all their animals be ours? Only let us agree with them, and they will live among us" (Gen. 34:23).

---

1   Cam Miller. "The Physics of Pain or Gallstones for the Soul." *The Subversive Preacher*. October 20, 2013. Retreived from http://subversivepreacher.com/2013/10/20/the-physics-of-pain-or-gallstones-of-the-soul/

And so the issues of living together were never put on the table and seen for what they were. The list would have been long: who is your God? Monotheism. Laws. Promises from God. Who did the land belong to? Would negotiating these issues have helped? Or would this discussion have prevented both sides from ever agreeing to joint living arrangements in that land? What do you think?

In marital engagements, before the couple say the powerful three words (I love you!), shouldn't they have a few fights first? Shouldn't they test whether they can approach and resolve conflict or will soon develop the habit of avoiding it? Like a man in the ad saying: "Here I am in this bathtub, watching the sun set, and you are in the bathtub next to me, and we are supposedly waiting for the 'time to be right;' but as a matter of fact, it is always 'right' for me and doesn't seem to be 'ever' right for you!"

Besides sex as an issue for conflict, there is money and who pays the bills and who does what work to keep the house clean and the refrigerator full and the clothes fresh and ironed. "Are these habits we have fallen into OK with you?" a spouse might ask. "Or are you just doing these things because you KNOW I don't know how to cook and you hate the way I make a bed, since I never used to make mine at home?"

Cam Miller raises, but does not dwell on, a good point: when does too much conflict render you dysfunctional? In the days of our government's shutdown, weren't the issues clearly on the table? Both sides KNEW what the other side wanted and believed in. But they just couldn't go there. There was no room for compromise, only capitulation. Only the threat of chaos made SOME legislators change their votes to end the impasse.

Is this suggesting that some conflicts are unresolvable? Or is it pointing to the necessity of leading combatants to WANT to resolve the conflict? Of course, there is a whole science of conflict resolution and career diplomats, mediators, marriage counselors and other professionals who would have good advice for us, if we wanted to hear it.

The New Interpreters' Study Bible reminds us that Jacob was really angry that his two sons had reacted with such deception and violence against the Canaanites. In effect, Jacob cut those two out of his will by not including their names in his final blessing before he died. The Study Bible states that the story is meant to dissuade the reader from solving conflict by violence.

But we return to Cam Miller's point: some conflict is healthy, productive and is avoided at the peril of killing future communication, not to mention deep love. Some conflict should not be ignored, and confronting it, bringing it up, hashing through it will be extremely painful but need not be violent. It can remove old bandages from wounds that have gotten infected and festered. With the right treatment, those wounds can heal.

Jesus is a model. He plowed straight into conflict. He did not return the violence he met. He said "Put away your sword" to Peter, who cut off the soldier's ear, and then reached out to that same soldier with a healing touch. Can we be led to want a similar stance, to stand like Samson between the two pillars of not avoiding conflict and yet doing that out of a sincere desire and a growing skill to be peacemakers?

From Rape to Murder:
1 Kings 18:17-40

We went to a memorial service recently, of a beloved widow who lived a full life, but died rather suddenly. Each of her four children spoke. They all told different stories. Although there were commonalities, each adult son or daughter had his or her own perspective on what was an important memory. It took all four to round out the picture of who this person was.

And so we get to this difficult passage from the First Book of Kings. According to the book itself (First Second Kings were obviously one book broken into two scrolls), the authors had various sources, like a preacher giving a eulogy, who interviews surviving family members, but may also look at the internet or at church or community news articles and archives. Sources for the Books of Kings were the Books of the Annals of the Kings of Israel and the Annals for the Kings of Judah. Then there were the Book of the Acts of Solomon and sources dealing with the "Elijah Cycle" and the "Elisha Cycle," Isaiah, and other prophets.

The children at the memorial service were making a point with their stories—they were giving evidence that a very good woman had lived and had done much to improve this world. Similarly, the authors of Kings, according to Walter Harrelson, "selected, combined, and arranged the written and oral traditions of Israel and Judah to express their theological understanding of their histories."[1]

We can imagine someone preaching a eulogy from the theological viewpoint that "everything has a purpose," or—as one of my Spiritual Reflections on biblicaljoe.com is titled: "There Are No Coincidences." Indeed, that reflection, written some years ago, refers to this very passage in the First Book of Kings!

What's difficult about this passage, of course, is not that Elijah—

[1]   Walter Harrelson. New Interpreter's Study Bible. (Nashville: Abingdon Press, 2003) 479.

God's favored prophet—causes fire to come from heaven and consume an offering that has been doused three times with water—but that he has the crowds who then come to believe that his God is the "right" God, bring him the 450 prophets of the "wrong" God so that he can slit their throats. –A mass murder, right there in the Bible! –No moral comment, no justification offered, no sanctions afterward…all dead.

What are we to make of this? It was a time when the theological understanding was that illness and disease were the consequences of sin; epilepsy was a sign that you were possessed by a demon; blasphemy was punishable by death, and there was no greater crime than infidelity to the "right" God. There was no separation of church and state. Infidels did not deserve to live, especially since they were spreading the cult of Baal, the great false god.

So Elijah, in provoking this confrontation between himself and Jezebel, which because of there being no separation of church and state, was engaging in a battle fought between the God of Israel (represented by Elijah) and the Canaanite God Baal (represented by the prophets). The thinking was that all of the calamities, droughts, and genocidal attacks against Israel were BECAUSE of the infidelity of the King and his wife and their promotion of the Canaanite religion. After all, Ahab designated priests for their shrines and Jezebel cultivated a large group of their prophets.   Elijah was acting to save his nation from destruction.   For him, the covenant meant that God was on his side and would save Israel and give the Israelites the land God had promised to Abraham and Jacob.

In that culture, at that time, death was the only fitting punishment for idolatry.

This is not the way Jesus treated non-believers. He deepens our theological understanding by his teaching about enemies, and by his treatment of those deemed sinners or 'unclean' or 'foreigners'or widows.

The question is whether or not our theological understanding has changed, grown and matured? Perhaps the MOST difficult part of reading today this passage from Kings is to probe where we are in our theological understanding. Do we still believe that certain people who have done certain things deserve to be killed? Do we believe that everyone should buy a gun so that, if sufficiently threatened, they can use it to kill someone? Do we still believe that God will condemn some people to eternal conscious torment in a place we call hell? Do we, in fact, curse people who have seriously offended us and pray that they go there? Do we insist on the right to stockpile weapons of mass destruction and to drop bombs, fire rockets, and engage in war those who are a threat to our national security?

These and similar questions are not easy to deal with. Some of us wrestle, wrestle with them, as Jacob did with the divine presence in Genesis 32. We wrestle with such passages to squeeze out compassion, as Karen Armstrong advocated in the TED award that inaugurated her Charter of Compassion.[2]

What theological understanding makes you act differently when someone attacks you or your loved ones or your property? Those who are true pacifists have an answer for this, I'm sure. Maybe we should learn what it is, especially those of us who follow a man who let himself be executed when he could have raised an army to prevent it. What theological understanding did he have? And what are our favorite stories about him?

The violence stopped with him on that Friday we call "Good," and it also stopped with those early martyrs who were killed for following his way. Then later, when religion was married to the might of the empire, the violence was initiated and justified by those who proclaimed him as Savior but felt duty- bound to kill those who did not believe. With what theological understanding do we tell that story?

In textweek.org, Nanette Williams discusses what it means for Elijah to be a murderer, and what the passage says about how the author perceived God. She feels it best to leave the questions the passages rais-

2   Karen Armstrong. "My Wish: The Charter of Compassion." *TED2008.* February, 2008. Retreived from https://www.ted.com/talks/karen_armstrong_makes_her_ted_prize_wish_the_charter_for_compassion.

es unanswered. One of her commentators noted how we are amidst all kinds of thieves, liars, addicts, criminals, deviates and murderers, and yet we have to live among them, attend to their needs, even love them.

Then I remembered Moses was a murderer, right. And yet God chose him to a most important role in the history of the Israelites. And I combine that realization with Richard Rohr's meditation:

> *God's one-of-a-kind job description is that God actually uses our problems to lead us to the full solution. God is the perfect Recycler, and in the economy of grade, nothing is wasted, not even our worst sins nor our most stupid mistakes. God does not punish our sins, but uses them to soften our hearts toward everything.*[3]

Isn't that what God did with Elijah?

3   Rohr. "Daily Meditations." November 2, 2013.

Let Me Help You?
John 13:5-17

When you ask people what passages in Scripture are "difficult" for them, it quickly becomes clear that what's judged problematic for one person is not at all difficult for another. That may be the case with this week's choice, the washing of the disciples' feet passage in John's Gospel. There is one line in that passage that is curious and at least needs unpacking, if not "solving." The line is: "If I do not wash you, you have no part with Me" (John 13:7).

Why would Jesus say that? It was already apparent that he was turning the concept of leadership on its head—stating that the master should be the servant and giving these leaders the role of servanthood as their responsibility. He was quoted in Luke as saying: "The kings of the Gentiles lord it over them; and those who have authority over them are called Benefactors. But it is not this way with you, but the one who is the greatest among you must become like the youngest, and the leader like the servant…I am among you as the one who serves" (Luke 22:25-27).

So why did he say that to Peter? He had already made his point that the leader in the new community has to be willing to get his hands dirty and smell the foul smells of dirty feet and wash the grime away . Was Jesus' reply about NOT letting Peter keep him in the "master" role (because that would indicate that Peter didn't "get" the essential structure of Jesus' Way)? Or was it something more?

Receiving help, allowing yourself to be taken care of, ministered to—is not always easy, especially for those of us who have never accepted charity, who always decline offers to help. We don't like to be put in the position of NEEDING anything. We don't like to feel indebted. It hurts our egos to feel we can no longer take care of ourselves or accomplish what we used to. We like to be in control.

And so I wonder if Jesus is making the point to Peter, who would deny him three times and run away like they all did, except for John and his Mother and her friends, with this gesture and these words that implied: "Peter, you don't yet know the depth of your cowardice and fear in the face of violence and evil. And you have to let me help you, to let me heal you, to let me bring you back from that betrayal so you will not despair. I want you to continue to be my follower and to lead others to follow me."

The counter-intuitive relationship here goes something like this: We have been taught that we need to acknowledge our sin, repent of it, and then give it up, fix it, refrain from that addiction or bad behavior. We need to make up for it, offer restitution, like Zaccheus running at the mouth: "If I have defrauded anyone, I am paying it back fourfold."

But this passage falls into the world view that suggests that our stance must be to let God USE our sins and addictions for God's own purposes. We let him heal us from within so that we can move forward on his way. We don't fall into the trap that we can do it all—that all we need is a little knowledge, a pinch of motivation, and some time to do it ourselves (i.e. to save ourselves).

There is a difficult passage after this, of course, when Jesus says he does not speak of all of you because he knows the ones he had chosen (Jn. 13:18), but that's for next time. For now, anyone who has relapsed, who has tried and failed a hundred times, who feels trapped, who can't find the will nor the motivation to WANT to be healed, the thought that opening oneself to God's work, to let Him/Her USE your problem, sin, addiction to heal you and carry you forward into His/Her arms can be quite consoling, and good news indeed. But does it mean that we don't have to do anything? That we can wallow in the mud?

Well, there is the need to take off one's sandals and offer one's feet. There is the letting Him/Her do it. There is the not wanting to wallow in the mud because some part of us knows it is NOT a good place to be. There is the desire to be transformed when we know transformation is possible.

Are You Chosen? Am I?

The difficult line in John 13, in Jesus' words after he has washed his disciples' feet is: "What I say is not said of all, for I know the kind of men I chose." Right after that, he hands a morsel dipped in wine to Judas and tells him to be quick in what he is about to do.

This idea of being "chosen" by God has deep roots and many examples in Scripture. Isaiah has God fondly refer to "Israel, whom I have chosen" (44:1). Peter calls his early Christian readers "a chosen race, a royal priesthood, …a people [God] claims for his own" (1 Peter 2:9). There are detailed, exciting and deeply emotional stories of people being chosen to carry out God's plan of salvation. Think of the people chosen for the covenant relationship with God: Abraham, Isaac, Jacob. Sometimes they had their names changed: Abram to Abraham; Jacob to Israel. If you were chosen, your status would be passed on to your children. There are careful records of genealogies to show who this favored status included.

Think of the choice of Moses to lead the most portentous deliverance in history; or how about the choice of his brother Aaron and his sister Miriam? Think about the call to Samuel and the Judges, and Samuel's anointing of that great King, David, son of Jesse. Women figured into the plan as well: Sarah and Rachel and Ruth and Deborah just to name a few.

Then there were the prophets, with some pretty dramatic choices in Elijah and Elisha, Isaiah and Jeremiah. How about the choice of Job to be tested by the Accuser to the depths of his being? In the New Testament, we have Zachary's story and Elizabeth's and Mary's and Joseph's, John the Baptist's and Jesus himself. In his time, Jesus chooses his disciples and apostles. After his death, they chose Stephen and the deacons, and Saul—sprawling on the ground, unable to see, the voice of Jesus ringing in his ears–got chosen in spite of his venomous actions toward Jesus's followers.

Are WE chosen? By whom and for what? Do we want to 'be among their number, when the saints go marching in' to eternal life and happiness? In his "priestly prayer," was Jesus talking about US when he said: "For these I pray—not for the world but for these you have given me, for they are really yours" (John 17:9)?

Don't we imagine that we are chosen for some special purpose, some special mission? Isn't Paul implying that the Corinthians are chosen because they have different gifts, each one a benefit for the community (1 Cor. 12)? Don't we imagine we are like Isaiah, responding to his horrific vision of having his lips burned with an ember from the fire, when we sing: "Here I am, Lord…Send me!" (Is. 6:8)?

I think the answer is yes, with this twist: the Jewish people were NOT chosen to be superior to others, to lord it over others, to be saved while others were damned. Most of those chosen had some serious character flaws or were the humblest of people ("He has regarded the lowliness of his handmaid," Mary exclaimed in her hymn). Being chosen required some cooperation.

We are chosen for others. Maybe as pinch hitters, designated batters, replacements, off the bench or front and center. The choosing is not about us individually. We may not be able to mess It up or thwart the plan. Jonah tried that. Didn't work. There is a force involved, a green fuse, a freshness deep down things BECAUSE, as GM Hopkins boldly and baldly states from his deep faith: "The Holy Ghost over the bent world broods…With warm breath and with—Ah!—bright wings!"[1]

---

1   "God's Grandeur." Gerard Manley Hopkins: Poems and Prose (Penguin Classics, 1985).

Infancy Narratives

Very few would put these two gospel passages down as "difficult passages in Scripture." After all, what can be difficult about the birth of a baby and the fulfillment of prophecies that had survived through almost a thousand years?

Besides, we have all known hard times when external forces like storms and natural disasters, or even minor occurrences such as a broken water pipe or a tax audit have thrown our homes and households into a chaos that may take days, weeks, months or years to overcome and get beyond. Many of us have set out on a long journey without much planning and found motels full and had to settle for shabby accommodations or rooms formerly used by smokers. A few of us have possibly slept in our cars.

John's Gospel doesn't have an infancy narrative, but the first words of his gospel epitomize an astonishing problem here: He claims and millions of people after him have believed, that the Word that existed before creation has now come to join that creation—not as its creator, but as one of its billions of births.

John and the other evangelists knew of writings, or sacred texts, that seemed to apply to this birth and this life, to this Jesus born in Bethlehem and raised in Nazareth.

There were lots of creation stories floating around when the author of Genesis put his quill to parchment. We can imagine people wanting to know: where did all of this come from? Sit outside your dwelling on a clear, frosty night. Where did these stars originate? Why do they move and some seem to gather in recognizable shapes, like dippers and swans and a belt with a dagger hanging from it?

In fact, where did WE come from and how to we fit in? Speaking of daggers, why do we so often wound and kill each other. The author of Genesis explains this. God made it. It was all good. We lived in a peaceable kingdom until the flaw that was always in us—the untamable desire for knowledge, power and pleasure brought us to know hatred, pain, and death.

Who would believe such a story? Does it make sense? And how about this Creator who wouldn't let his creatures divorce Him/Her, but kept coming after them with help and promises and an unquenchable desire to be loved and to love?

The gospel writers looked back on the whole panoply of those promises and brought some of them forward to apply to their time and ours: This is he who was foretold in Genesis and Isaiah and typified in Exodus and Samuel and Kings and sung about in the Psalms. They wrote their stories with these ancient promises and texts ringing in their ears.

Who would believe such stories? –Maybe those who haven't given up hope yet; those who have experienced in themselves and in the beauty and the awfulness of nature a divine presence, a guiding hand, a force moving humanity along toward some transformation, some peaceable future; and above all, those who have watched people die—even their loved ones—and refuse to believe, who know in their hearts, that their loved ones' spirits could not be trashed and gone forever.

All creation groans (Rom. 8:22)—often with misery, but sometimes with pure joy and laughter. We are so grateful for these stories that say it so well. We are not abandoned and alone, even when we cannot imagine the size of the universe or the distance of the stars.

Laborers in the Vineyard:
a Difficult Passage?

After a pause for six weeks of meetings, we can now go back to our "Difficult Passages in Scripture" theme. Does this passage from Matthew 20 surprise you?

I want to bring several sources to bear on this Scripture. The first, of course, is the scripture itself, and its commentary in *The New Interpreters Study Bible*. The second is this poem called "Wild Geese" by Mary Oliver, winner of both a National Book Award and a Pulitzer Prize for Poetry that many modern spiritual writers are quoting these days:

You do not have to be good.

You do not have to walk on your knees

For a hundred miles through the desert, repenting.

You only have to let the soft animal of your body

love what it loves.

Tell me about your despair, yours, and I will tell you mine.

Meanwhile the world goes on.

Meanwhile the sun and the clear pebbles of the rain

are moving across the landscapes,

over the prairies and the deep trees,

the mountains and the rivers.

Meanwhile the wild geese, high in the clean blue air,

are heading home again.

Whoever you are, no matter how lonely,

the world offers itself to your imagination,

calls to you like the wild geese, harsh and exciting —

over and over announcing your place

in the family of things.[1]

The third is a reflection from Cam Miller, in his "Subversive Preacher" blog.[2]

The fourth is this poignant writing for the Sacred-Scared Project by Glennon Doyle where she comments that we all must show up in our "beautiful, messy glory."[3]

I'll add a fifth, from the edgy book *Pastrix: The Cranky, Beautiful Faith of a Sinner and Saint*, by Nadia Bolz-Weber.[4] I could probably add a sixth, if you have the time to listen to Joan Chittister's TED talk.[5] And finally, a seventh, the quote from Rumi:

Come, come, whoever you are,

Wanderer, worshiper, lover of leaving—

It doesn't matter.

Ours is not a caravan of despair.

Come, even if you have broken your vows

A hundred times

Come, come again, come.[6]

I. But let's start with the Scripture:

The passage is pretty well known and has a standard interpretation, brought about by the words of Jesus at the end.   God's empire is

1   Mary Oliver. "Wild Geese." *New and Selected Poems.* (Boston: Beacon Press, 2004).

2   Cam Miller. "The Pulpit: Sermons." *The Subversive Preacher.* February 19, 2014. Retrieved from https://subversivepreacher.org/subversivepreaching-sermons-preacher-helps.

3   Glennon Doyle. "Our Sacred-Scared Day One." *The Momastery.* February 19, 2014. Retrieved from http://momastery.com/blog/2014/02/19/sacred-scared-day-one/#sthash.vPj5HdH8.dpuf.

4   Nadia Bolz Weber. *Pastrix: The Cranky, Beautiful Faith of a Sinner and Saint.* (Nashville: Jericho Books, 2014).

5   Joan Chittister. "TEDTalk." *TEDx Talk in Fact and Faith.* Dec. 9, 2012. Retrieved from https://www.youtube.com/watch?v=575V-CgiVOE.

6   Rumi quoted in Sy Safransky. A Book of Quotations. (Berkeley: North Atlantic Books, 2012) 67.

NOT like the empires people are used to. It challenges the way we're used to act and are acted upon by our superiors. NISB says these were probably poor day laborers without any artisan skills. They worked for a denarius, which assured them of, at best, a subsistence existence. The availability of workers throughout the day suggests an oversupply and rampant unemployment. The landowner uses wages to unify rather than divide (rich—poor gap). The Interpreter's Bible says that verse 15 should be translated: "Is you eye evil because I am good?" I.e., he wants them to see in a new way and adopt his social structure. But, we shakily ask, is this meant to be economic theory and advice? What would such a practice do to capitalism?

At first glance, this passage seems to be a simple story about being generous. The take-away could be only: Be generous! But we know that in our present culture, any employer that would try this would quickly find him or herself in trouble with the union and probably in court, because of the manifest injustice to those who worked for long hours and were paid the same as those who worked for a fraction of that time. Ok, so the early birds agreed to that wageis ; but at the end of the day, it seems they had every right to complain ("I agreed to it not knowing that you were going to pay a full day's wages to those who only worked the last hour!") .

When we start drawing out implications, such as why Matthew included this story, and what Jesus was really saying, and was the land-owner a stand-in for God, and are we the workers—those of us who "get it" from the beginning and those of us who get up late and are clueless for most of the day? –Now we realize we are in deep water and many people will caution us not to take our interpretations too far (such as to suggest that Jesus was once again upending the social and political power structures).

II. Now, in order to see how the other five sources fit with this scripture, I'll move to the fifth, and tell you something about *Pastrix*, the autobiogrphay of Weber, who grew up in Denver, Colorado and after years as a stand-up comic, a depressed alcoholic, and an iconoclastic teenager who also had to contend with Graves disease from age twelve to age sixteen, with her eyes bulging out of her face—after all of this, she felt herself called to be a pastor to the down and out, the marginal, and people whom the 'righteous' do not usually accept—and a Lutheran Pastor, to boot. "Pastrix" is an insulting term for a female pastor.

Two things I want to draw from this book: one, her comments about grace,[7] and then the passage that tells about her first sermon, to a group of LGBTQ people after the ELC changed its mind about homosexuality and allowed ordination of gays in a permanent relationship.[8]

Concerning Grace, she points out that Grace is not God being an all-forgiving Good Guy, but "It's God saying, 'I love the world too much to let your sin define you and be the final word. I am a God who makes all things new."[9] And then when she applies the concept to the parable about the laborers in the vineyard, she maintains: "This is exactly, when it comes down to it, why most people do not believe in grace. It is [flippin] offensive!"[10]

This is, she maintained in her sermon, NOT a parable about workers, but a parable about the landowner (God). "What makes this the kingdom of God…is the fact that the trampy landowner couldn't manage to keep out of the marketplace. He goes back and back and back, interrupting lives…coming to get his people. Grace tapping us on the shoulder."[11]

Mary Oliver says: "you do not have to be good…the world calls to you."[12] Rumi says: "Come, even if you have broken your vows a hundred times."[13] Doyle says:

> *Everybody is the same. No one has it all figured out and No one ever will. We just gotta show up for our dreams and each other before*

7   Weber, 48.

8   Ibid., 55.

9   Ibid., 49.

10   Ibid., 55.

11   Ibid., 57.

12   Oliver, "Wild Geese."

13   Rumi.

we're ready. We can be scared and still show up. We can be complete-
ly UNHEALED and still show up. We must just show up in all our
beautiful, messy glory. Because all the good and all the beautiful in
the world is created by people who show up before they're ready.[14]

Rev. Cam Miller says: "..not only do we not have to be good…we do
not have the option to be good."[15]

And: The whole idea that a god capable of creating such exquisite
and delicate beauty as evidenced in the Cosmos, also operates as a parsi-
monious punisher of human foibles, is childish in the extreme.

The fact that Christian theology has not moved beyond Old World
notions of original sin, heaven and hell, salvation for the good and eternal punishment for the bad, God causing Jesus to die on the cross and
in so doing somehow saving us from our badness (Atonement) is tragic.
There is so much at the heart of Christianity, in the Gospels themselves
that reject these ideas.

Finally (whew!), Joan Chittister, in her powerful TEDx talk stated
that we all finally come to the realization that perfection is "perfectly
impossible." She claims that we are at a crossover moment in time;
That whatever was considered true up to this time will no longer be
considered true;   That the classical worldview that has God personally
creating everything, with hierarchy built in and the male as a pinnacle
of creation has been blown apart by the theories of the big bang and
evolution. The new view is that God's creation is a work in progress and
we are given the responsibility of making choices for new and better life.
Failure is a part of this, but we can learn from failure cooperate with
God to choose new growth and help bring about a better world.

Whether we find this God at the beginning of the day, the middle of
the day or the end of the day doesn't matter. The important thing is that
we find him/her and accept his/her invitation to get to work!

I know that there are those out there who could find thousands

---

14   Doyle, "Our Sacred-Scared Day One."
15   Miller. "The Pulpit: Sermons."

of sources that reaffirm the classical view of creation and a traditional image of God. The question is whether these sound like good news, are life-giving, and give hope for our planet?

"You Have Heard That It Was Said, But I Say…"

This passage is difficult because Jesus says that he has come to fulfill the law, not to abolish it (nor the Prophets). But then he goes on to quote the law about murder, adultery, oaths, retaliation and enemies and goes way beyond it in most cases. "You have heard that it was said, but what I say to you is…"

Jesus seems to be on the side of the conservative interpreters of the Torah, stating that not one smallest part of a letter of it should ever be changed. The Jewish scholar, Amy Jill Levine, reminds us that not everything in the Torah is a law, and that way back at the time of Hillel, Jews believed that there was an oral Torah and a written Torah, and both had equal value. But the one can be interpreted by the other. The Hebrew word for law (nomos) can be translated "teaching" and so gives further credence that not everything in the Torah, whether written or oral, has the force of law.[1]

Still, Jesus seems to be pointing the way to a higher standard of conduct. He didn't seem to have much tolerance for external observances, rituals or practices that were not accompanied by an interior purity of intention. He knew that what comes out of our character and motivation and instincts means more than what we profess to believe. He knew how difficult it is for us to accomplish even the most unselfish-looking deeds without having mixed motives for doing so.

For those who celebrate or know about Ash Wednesday, with ashes so recently traced on our foreheads and the accompanying words assaulting our ears: "Remember that you are dust and unto dust you shall return," perhaps we have a context in which to interpret this difficult passage from Matthew's Gospel.

Our lives go so fast—we are old before we realize the years have

---

1   See Amy Jill Levine. The Jewish Annotated New Testament. (Oxford: Oxford University Press, 2011).

passed. We can't believe the ages of our children and grandchildren.
You never thought you would live to be forty, and then suddenly find
yourself in your sixties or seventies or eighties! Ashes indeed. I know
this is a little far out, but what if Jesus, in these words recorded by Matthew, were trying to teach us something about life and death?

We are, are we not, used to playing up certain laws in Scripture and
ignoring others. I was in a discussion group of teachers just the other
day, and they were complaining about how little respect students seem
to have these days. They don't respect each other, nor do they respect
their elders, their parents, their political leaders nor people who have
a LOT more education, resources, and knowledge than they do! Why,
they think nothing of calling their professors by their first names! In-
civility seems to be increasing by the day. Road rage is common. Bad
language crowds out polite speech.

These are not new accusations, of course, and our own parents and
grandparents would probably remember being scandalized by the youth
of THEIR day. What a step up in ethical behavior, don't you think, if
people would just observe the Ten Commandments!

But then, let's look at the standards Jesus is holding up to us in Matthew 5, right after he has enunciated the Beatitudes. What a different
world it would be if all of us observed the Beatitudes! But in compar-
ison with the Ten Commandments, they are mostly ignored, even by
religious people. And that may be because they are nearly impossible
for us to live by, just as it is nearly impossible to live by the words in this
"difficult passage."

Think about it: Who does turn the other cheek? Who gives a thief
or a beggar more than he wants to have? Who walks that extra mile
and never harbors a lustful desire, never uses abusive language, never
dislikes someone to the point of hatred, and always says 'yes' when he or
she means 'yes?' Who?

Lent is a good time to try all of these things, but we all know that
our chances of failing some or all of these benchmarks are very high.

Don't bet too much money on anyone's total success here.

I understand that some American Indian tribes see life as a spiral instead of a staircase. We are where we are in the folds of that spiral. We may take one step forward and two steps back, but that's okay. What if God is continuing to create and humanity is continuing to evolve as is everything else in this universe?

Nothing is lost. Whereas our news reporters delight in finding crime and selfishness and graft and political scandals, what if God is an investigative reporter looking for goodness and for instances of people approaching the standards of this difficult passage? Even we, myopic as we sometimes are, can find lots of examples of extreme generosity, kindness, forgiveness and compassion, self-sacrifice and even heroism. We've managed some of them ourselves, haven't we?

Some people routinely "pay it forward," volunteer to take day-old bread to hunger centers, look out after older people living alone, travel to countries where they share their knowledge and skills, teaching people to raise fish, sew, plant. And many more people just "show up" at their daily duties, performing these as well and as cheerfully as possible, even those involving an angry child or a high maintenance spouse.

And what if this same God who knows we most often miss our target standards and even in Lent cannot lose as many pounds as we need to—what if that God cherishes this creation and helps, prods, motivates and challenges it to throw off its encumbrances and dance!

Passages That I Hate

I want to pose a question that you might find too disrespectful to answer: Are there any passages in Scripture that you absolutely HATE? I have a number, especially those that have been used as a weapon against other people in God's creation. But I suppose my all-time favorite to hate is that one from Genesis, when Abraham is asked to take his only son up the mountain and kill him (Genesis 22:2). [I can't even stand to post the most common depictions of it].

I learned many of the interpretations of this passage as I've wrestled with it over the years. Paul uses it to point out Abraham's great faith (Romans 4). Or you can view it as the supreme test to see if you are obedient to the Almighty and can count on His goodness no matter what He requires you to do. Then there's the real possibility that this passage was put into Genesis to call an end to child sacrifice to gods who had altars in the high places. Christian writers were eager to point out that God's son was not spared like Abraham's was—because of our terrible sins that needed washing away with blood.

But once my wife and I had a firstborn son, this passage went right to the top of my all-time hate list. I could understand the terrible possibility that something might happen to him. I used to listen to him breathe at night in his basinet, just to be certain he was okay. Being conceived, born, and growing up are all miraculous, given the number of things that can go wrong. I could only hope my faith would be strong enough if the unthinkable happened. But being told to end his life as if the answer were needed for some high stakes loyalty test—well, that would be too much for me. I hesitate to write, but it's true, that I can't believe in a God who would ask that.

So, you may legitimately wonder: Well, then, how can you believe in a God who requires His own Son to suffer a criminal's death so that YOU might live eternally in happiness, instead of in perpetual torment?

To answer that, let me explain what all this has to do with the

Transfiguration, the story in Matthew 17 and in all three synoptic gospels:

I always thought the Transfiguration was a great story! It's so visual!: there's a mountain, a transformation that involves Jesus's body and his clothes, there are appearances of two prophets long dead (well one of them, at least), and there is this thunderous voice from heaven claiming Jesus as the Son of God whom everyone should listen to. What could be the problem with this wondrous scene?

So I was shocked when an episcopal priest of my acquaintance declared this passage the one he hated (I think he actually says "disliked")! He hates it because if it is taken as history, it is a way of telling people of all other religions and beliefs (Hindus, Moslems, Jews, for example) that Jesus is the only one to be listened to. This passage can be one more log for the fire of Anti-Semitism.

How do you get out of this way of thinking—that God only loves those who listen to Jesus? You have to think about what Matthew is saying to his Jewish audience. If you keep thinking that this story means that Jesus was replacing Moses and Elijah or—what the heck—everyone important in Jewish history, then you'd have to be the kind of exclusionist that Jesus never was!

But you CAN accept this story (and, I suppose, that one about Abraham) as an emblem of what happens when you encounter God. You're thrown off your feet (or your game). You cannot resolve the experience by thinking about it. You rather stand before it like Moses did in his own Transfiguration in Exodus 24. It is a burning bush experience. It can open your heart as if with a not-too-sharp can opener; and you have to acknowledge, like Job, that you haven't a clue, that the God who created this universe is bigger than you are, and that the best thing you can ever do is to keep believing in Him/Her, even when God acts like a moving target and won't let you build a tent that you can crawl into and get comfortable.

Women Should Be Silent!

If we could land on one book of Scripture that would convince us that Scripture is NOT all of a piece, and that there are many variations in genre, authorship, and authenticity through the ages, it's this letter to Timothy. Those who shy away from making distinctions among the books may have to accept some of the responsibility for what 1 Timothy has done to women through the centuries, especially this second chapter.

The issue of the roles of women in our contemporary world was brought home to me in a blog warning that climate change is going to affect ALL of us, no matter how far away we are from the melting glaciers. According to the United Nations, "We know that in 38 of the 48 countries surveyed by the United Nations in a 2010 report, women (over 15 years old) are responsible for searching and collecting drinking water. The harder it is to access it, the further they will have to walk, the worse their health will be, and the less time they will have to educate themselves."[1]

Luckily, we have scholars such as John Dominic Crossan, who distinguish between a radical Paul (in his seven authentic letters), a liberal Paul, and a conservative Paul. As Crossan puts it, "someone was cleaning up Paul" from his radical notions.[2]

Scholars are convinced that Paul didn't even WRITE 1 Timothy, although it has been the cause of much dislike of Paul by women.

Chapter two of 1 Timothy is fascinating in how it has been (and still is) interpreted. Amy Jill Levine reminds us that the delay in the Second Coming of Jesus, which was the issue in Paul's Letters to the Thessalonians, led the scribes writing in the name of Paul to support the status quo; namely, that women were to find their salvation in having

1   The UN Millenium Development Goals. Retrieved from http://www.un.org/millenniumgoals/.

2   John Dominic Crossan. "The Search for the Historical Paul." Retrieved from http://youtu.be/txdUXCY0clU.

children and their husbands were to rule the household, in the patriarchal culture (and in popular moral treatises) of the time.

Levine even writes, in her notes on chapter two of 1 Timothy: "The view that women are subordinate to men and that the subordination derives from Genesis [note that the New Interpreter's Study Bible calls 1 Timothy 2:14 a 'somewhat forced' reading of Genesis] appears in later Jewish circles and is native to some rabbinic understanding of womanhood…"[3] When I remind my wife that Scripture says she should be subject to me, she gives me that look that promises: "In your dreams!" Rightly so: we are partners who love each other dearly, and hierarchy is not even an issue. In this, we may be following the teachings of Jesus in the Gospels, since he often turned hierarchy on its head.

In a study of Paul that has been a staple of seminaries, colleges and universities for 25 years, Calvin Roetzel writes: "In this new age all barriers that divide the human family are removed, and all obstacles to fulfillment are torn down. Although Paul nowhere attacks prevailing customs that assign women inferior roles in society, he obviously believes they are full partners 'in Christ.' When one treats women as full and equal citizens in the kingdom of God, it is difficult to hold disparaging views of them."[4]

Garry Wills, in his *What Paul Meant*, devotes a whole chapter to "Paul and Women" and much of it is devoted to Paul's positive relationships to such women as Junia, Prisca, Phoebe, and "the women prophets." Wills acknowledges that in that patriarchal culture of Paul's time, it was impossible "to shed every remnant of sexism," but "Paul gives every kind of honor to the women he works with."[5]

A fascinating look into what it would mean for a woman to take seriously what the Bible teaches about women can be found in Rachel Held Evans' book, *A Year of Biblical Womanhood*. The subtitle will give you the idea: "How a Liberated Woman Found Herself Sitting on Her

---

3   Levine, 432.
4   Calvin Roetzel. *The Letters of Paul.* (Louisville, KY: Westminster John Knox Press, 2009), 3.
5   Garry Wills. *What Paul Meant.* (New York: Penguin Books, 2007) 98.

Roof, Covering Her Head, and Calling Her Husband 'Master.'" Fortunately, she didn't try to observe all that the Bible seems to demand of a woman at once. She emphasized certain requirements each month. In August, she observes 1 Timothy 2:11-14 by avoiding teaching or speaking. Since she already had speaking engagements scheduled, she found a way around this stricture by following the interpretation of the founder of the Council on Biblical Manhood and Womanhood, who wrote: "The Bible is clear that women shouldn't teach and have authority over men. In context, I think this means that women shouldn't be the authoritative teachers of the church." That left room for a speaking engagement here and there. Then she checked into a Trappist monastery where she could observe a silent retreat. Needless to say, she has an understanding husband!

Perhaps a way to swim free of the many places in the Biblical culture that attempt to force women to swim only in the pool of family life and children is to consider the viewpoint of blogger and author Sarah Bessy. Her blog is titled "In Which I Admit that I Didn't Like Paul." She called him "narrow-minded and bossy. He was snippy. As a feminist, I was suspicious of Paul. I even avoided his words in Scripture."

Yet as she was writing Jesus Feminist, she confesses that "I began to love Paul. Really, truly love him, as a brother." She moved through the passages she hated and considered Paul's full ministry. She discovered she hadn't really known him. Galatians (especially chapters 5 and 6) and wonderful passages in 1 and 2 Corinthians became her home and his words changed her attitude toward him forever. She found how he "praised and esteemed women in leadership in the Church, how he turned household codes within a patriarchal society on their head, how he used feminine metaphors, how he subverted the systems, how he passionately defended equality—the verses that used to clobber me began to embrace me."

She and all of us may become even more impressed if we come to agree with John Dominic Crossan that Paul didn't even WRITE Timothy and Titus and that 1 Corinthians 14:34-35 is an interpolation, according to those who should know. The radical Paul, whom Richard Rohr considers a mystical Paul, wanted all people to conclude: "In Christ there is neither Jew nor Gentile…neither male nor female…" (Gal. 3:28).   We are charged with transforming the world together!

Noah in the Movies

I suppose we should all be happy that the film industry is still making movies based on the Bible. It's another proof that those sacred books will endure as long as people inhabit the earth. The movie Noah has not received sterling reviews, but it is selling like a blockbuster just the same.

Now raise your hand if you think that the movie stays close to the details about the Flood in Genesis, chapters six through nine. Right. The movie runs over two hours. There are four chapters on which to base it. What's a director to do, if he or she wants hordes of people to buy tickets to see it? Why, interpret, or course, and embellish, and add characters and drama (oh, and use every special effect that has been invented)!

It's just extremely interesting to see how this age-old story is interpreted by 21st century writers and directors. And who's to say that the writer(s) of Genesis weren't doing the same thing as they wrote down this ancient story of a huge flood that wiped out a lot of life. Some of the early flood stories were found in the Epic of Atrahasis and in the Epic of Gilgamesh (see The New Interpreters' Study Bible, p. 16). There were others, usually following accounts of creation from chaos. With the flood, chaos is allowed to return.

As you read chapters 6-9 straight through, it is easy to discover that there are two stories in Genesis, conflated into one. Primary evidence for that is in the use of two different names for God in the original Hebrew. Biblical scholars have mapped out which verses belong to the "Yahwist" narrative and which one to the "Priestly" narrative. In the Yahwist version, it rains for 40 days and 40 nights; in the Priestly tradition, the flood lasts for a year. In the Yahwist, Noah is commanded to take seven pairs of clean animals, suitable for both eating and sacrifice; in the Priestly, only one pair of each is brought into the ark, whether clean or unclean. In the movie version, we understand that no real animals at all were used—just virtual ones.

Surely the liberties the director took with the movie, the addition of characters, including two granddaughters that Noah imagines he must sacrifice so that no humans would be left on earth; surely this makes the film controversial, and many critics have come forward, their complaints only adding to the hype and persuading more people to see it.

But the real controversy about biblical story of the Flood is that God gives up on his people and causes a natural disaster to wipe them out. Deserving as those humans were, God is portrayed as unmerciful. Then God makes a covenant with Noah after the Flood, ending with the promise that it will never happen again and here, possibly, is the creation of the rainbow, or at least its debut, the colorful bands that my granddaughter paints or wears every chance she gets.

And that gives away what makes this Flood story different from those other ancient epics. It is a human need to explain natural disasters. They are obviously beyond our power to control and so are attributed to a higher power. And we usually blame them on our sinfulness, our disobedience to the same higher power, just as Eve and Adam disobeyed in chapter three of this same book. What makes the Flood story in Genesis different, as Rob Bell has pointed out in his Blog series entitled "What Is the Bible," is that God "brings a rainbow and a promise and a covenant."[1] It's as if God recommits to us humans, makes an agreement with us, forgives us, (dare we say "loves" us?). The other stories end with everyone drowning and with the gods being satisfied. These four chapters teach us a whole new image of God, a whole different way of looking at and relating to God.

Rob Bell refuses to lose that point in arguments over whether the ark was big enough to hold two (or seven!) elephants. Such literalism, he maintains, misses "the point of the story. This story was a major leap forward in human consciousness, a breakthrough in how people conceived of the divine, another step toward a less violent, more relational understanding of the divine."

Floods continue to devastate and seem to be getting worse because

1   Rob Bell. "What is the Bible." Retrieved from http://robbellcom.tumblr.com/post/66199714202/what-is-the-bible-part-2-flood.

of our lack of will to control our emissions (the movie is criticized for making a similar point), but because of the inspired ending to the story of this disaster in Genesis, we can be so thankful for the rainbow!   And we can find whole groups of people who are determined to extend God's covenant to love and care for this earth we inhabit.

Subduing and Dominating

As those who study Scripture know, there are two accounts of creation in the Book of Genesis. In the one that appears in chapter 1,

> *God created man in his image; in the divine image he created him; male and female he created them. God blessed them, saying: 'Be fertile and multiply; fill the earth and subdue it. Have dominion over the fish of the sea, the birds of the air, and all the living things that move on the earth.' God also said; 'See, I give you every seed-bearing plant all over the earth and every tree that has seed-bearing fruit on it to be your food; and to all the animals of the land, all the birds of the air, and all the living creatures that crawl on the ground, I give all the green plants for food." And so it happened. God look at everything he had made, and he found it very good.* (Gen. 1:27-31).

In the second account, in chapter 2,

> *The Lord God formed man out of the clay of the ground and blew into his nostrils the breath of life, and so man became a living being* (Gen. 2:7)... *The Lord God then took the man and settled him in the garden of Eden to cultivate and care for it* (Gen. 2:15)... *The Lord God said: 'It is not good for the man to be alone. I will make a suitable partner for him." So the Lord God formed out of the ground various wild animals and various birds of the air, and he brought them to the man to see what he would call them; whatever the man called each of them would be its name* (Gen. 2: 18-19)... *So the Lord God cast a deep sleep on the man, and while he was asleep, he took out one of his ribs and closed up its place with flesh. The lord god then built up into a woman the rib that he had taken from the man* (Gen. 2:21-22).

Joan Chittister refers to this first book of the Bible to make the points that (1) they were undoubtedly written by a man from a male point of view; and both (2) hierarchy (man created first; woman second and subject to him; (3) and patriarchy are built in and have influenced history and culture ever since.[1]

Why in some countries are women and girls forbidden to become educated or even to drive? Isn't the argument that: it is the woman who attracts the man; it is the woman who gets pregnant, carries the child for months, and then gives birth. It is the woman who nurses the child and forms that first and closest of bonds with the child. It is the woman who towards the end of her pregnancy, has that urge "to nest;" and after she gives birth, she often is the one who sees to it that her family is taken care of in their nest/home. It often (usually in those days) falls to her to plan meals, cook (develop creative ways to deal with food), sew (or keep family in suitable clothing for the weather, culture, style, etc.), clean (especially laundry). In those early years, we are told, roles were defined for men as well. And there were always outstanding exceptions.

And so it seems at first glance that man was to subdue the earth and likewise subdue the female. He had naming rights. She had her place as his helpmate and he had his as her provider, warrior, defender and leader. Monogamy slowly evolved to become the preferred relationship and was accepted by nearly all cultures as the best institution to preserve a safe, secure and caring family.

What do you think of these descriptions? When we think of the difficult words in that first chapter of Genesis, they surely are the words "subdue" and "dominion." It's as if the writers, story tellers, myth makes of Genesis are putting these words in the head of Adam. He is to subdue and have dominion over all of creation, including his mate. And in the second chapter, when God is portrayed as feeling sorry for the man because he is alone, God first gives him animals and birds and almost as an afterthought, a female companion. Do you feel that readers and students of Genesis could derive these meanings from the text?

Joan Chittister maintains that when Galileo used a telescope and Darwin collected evidence that living things adapted to their changing environments by modifying themselves over centuries—a process we call evolution—things can never be the same; and we cannot go back to

---

1   See Chittister, TEDTalk.

these ancient and literal interpretations of Scripture.[2]

Largely led by males, we have tried dominating nature and subduing it according to our needs for food, pleasure and comfort. As we have succeeded, we were aggressive in acquiring more land and in inventing weapons for keeping our acquisitions safe from those humans who want what we have. In the western world, we have built our society around constant and necessary growth. We have allowed structures to develop that assured that some people have more resources than others. We claim that the upper classes have worked harder, were more intelligent, ingenious in investing, and careful about passing their wealth on to younger generations.

But now we may be at a tipping point: we may have subdued the earth to the point that it cannot recover and will soon be unable to sustain our burgeoning population. After the industrial revolution, we have kept making things without much thought for their disposal. We have dumped so much trash into the oceans that delight and sustain us, that it litters the bottom of every sea, and huge islands of plastic float about, often in dead zones that are bereft of oxygen and aquatic life.

We have taken to subduing others, to taking from others what we want. As our local media reported in May, 2014, there is so much gunfire in a certain section of Cleveland, that people no longer report it as a problem or even hear it.

The good news is that many people are awake to these issues and are actively doing something about them. They are steering away from a domination hierarchy to partnerships, beginning with loving partnerships between husbands and wives, men and women. This transition is NOT easy and is fraught with controversy. A surprising number of men and women are using their intelligence and influence (power) NOT to get or acquire more, but to GIVE. Instead of denying the results of scientific study, they are seeking to understand this data and its implications for our future. They are focusing on water, its distribution and purification; they are discovering and/or supporting initiatives for

---

2   Ibid.

stopping or at least lessening pollution of our air; they are making loans to people in third world countries who would never be able to start a business without them; they are devising new ways to be philanthropic that don't just throw money down the deep holes of poverty but "teach people how to fish" (or raise fish).

These are our new heroes and heroines, who travel to foreign countries with sewing machines, and music, and the wherewithal to build dwellings, schools and libraries. Whole organizations exist to promote peace and to practice it by reaching out to their former enemies in a posture of dialogue and cooperation.   In short, they are assisting in God's process of creation and in his process of evolution. They are calling everyone, inviting, challenging us to live as ONE. For Christians, this is to fulfill the law of Christ.

The Rich Young Man & Redistribution of Wealth

Isn't it interesting that Matthew puts this passage about the rich young man right after Jesus blesses the little children. Of course, these two events may have taken place on different days or even in different years, but switching from the innocent sweetness of little children to someone who has all the resources and sophistication that wealth and education can bring, must have taken a great deal of effort. I'm told that peace corps volunteers face this culture shock when they return from a third world country and re-enter a grocery store.

The wealthy man's question implies he is coming to grips with the fact that you can't take your riches with you when you die, and so he is wisely asking Jesus, the teacher and prophet, how he can obtain the one thing he doesn't yet have: eternal life. He asks what "good" he needs to do to merit eternal life.

When Jesus answers that there is only one who is good; namely, God, and then launches into a recitation of the commandments, the young man counters with what amounts to: "Whoa! I am good! I've kept all of these commandments." Jesus, instead of asking (as I would have): "Then why did you ask me 'Which ones?' when I said "keep the commandments?" Jesus must have looked at his clothing, his manner, the care he took of his skin, and then challenged him on the one thing he lacked in THIS life, detachment from his wealth.

As the young man went away grieving ("no eternal life for me—yi!"), Jesus commented on the extreme difficulty of getting into that eternal realm with your bags full of money.

Harrelson makes the assumption that since the man was wealthy, he could NOT have kept the commandments Jesus quoted; that in that era and culture, he got wealthy by exploiting others, being greedy, and depriving others of what he had accumulated. The NISB adds: "Contrary to elitist values that often despised the poor and blamed them for their poverty, wealth does not equate with virtue."[1] "Wealth has blinded him," NISB continues, "to unjust, hierarchical social relationships…To follow Jesus is to join a community that renounces domination based on birth and wealth, and where all are slaves (12:46-55; 20:24-28)…To live a life that deprives people of necessary resources, that maintains social inequities, makes it impossible to participate in God's empire. Repentance and restructured social and economic practices are necessary." Only God can effect that transformation.

Wow! Sounds like a call for the redistribution of wealth, doesn't it? Such a call would be fought with great vigor in the United States and labeled "Marxist" by many. The poor are, indeed, blamed for their poverty, their lack of education, and their living conditions. We who have wealth act as if we can earn eternal life with some generous contributions or by looking after our own. We even go so far as to regard our wealth as a gift from God, as evidence of His love for and approval of us.

When asking that same question—what must we do to gain eternal life—the ironical answer is "nothing…just desire it." More and more spiritual writers and thinkers are agreeing with Richard Rohr that grace is "the Divine Unmerited Generosity that is everywhere." As Rohr puts it in a Daily Meditation adapted from Job and the Mystery of Suffering and The Enneagram and Grace: 9 Journeys to Divine Presence:

"I would go so far as to call grace the primary revelation of the entire Bible. If you miss this message, all the rest is distorted and even destructive. I cannot emphasize this strongly enough.

The only perquisite for receiving the next grace is having received the previous one…Every moment is not obvious as God, as grace. It just looks like another ordinary moment. But your willingness to see it as gratuitous—as a free gift, as self-revelatory, as a possibility—allows it to be that way. God's hiding ceases. God and grace become apparent as a gift each moment. And those who learn how to receive gifts keep receiving further gifts."

---

1   Harrelson, 1781.

The question remains as to whether Jesus is calling for a redistribution of wealth. Or was that then, and this is now? After all, there have been quite a few changes in society, science, technology, food, population, communication and economies in two thousand years. But poverty still remains. The exploitation and destruction of the earth accelerates. Wealth is more and more concentrated among fewer and fewer people. Why would the wealthy ever want to redistribute wealth? –For eternal life? Didn't we just say it was free for those who desire it?

Ah. Maybe that's it: redistribution of wealth, freedom from it, letting go of it, is NECESSARY in order to even DESIRE eternal life. You don't want to be filled if you are already full. As poverty remains, so does the fact that wealth cannot be taken with you into that next realm of existence. In the U.S., the repeal of the estate tax tries to ensure that one's wealth will be passed on to the "right people." Pope Francis–no stranger to a knowledge about poverty–is calling for all of us to deal with it.

And so dealing with both wealth and poverty will take transformation, that's for sure, and it needs to start with me. It will take grace. It will take God.

A Communion Meditation
In February

I can imagine someone from, say, Arizona, at the Indians baseball training camp, sitting beside an escapee from Cleveland, and chuckling: "I understand at this time of year, you Clevelanders have only one thing on your mind." "Oh yeah?" the Clevelander would reply, "and what would that be?" –"Snow!"

I wondered if the Bible would offer some solution for this phenomenon we call snow (or some prayer to stop it!). I did a search and was totally surprised to find 24 references for snow. If I hadn't read of the recent snowstorm in the Middle East, I wouldn't have thought people in the desert would even know what snow was!

But, of course, there were the snows of Mt. Hermon and Mt. Lebanon, and talk of clothes and hands and hair being white as snow. I'm sure you are familiar with Robert Frost's famous poem, Fire and Ice:

Some say the world will end in fire,

Some say in ice.

From what I've tasted of desire

I hold with those who favor fire.

But if it had to perish twice,

I think I know enough of hate

To say that for destruction ice

Is also great

And would suffice.[1]

But then I found this other thing in the Bible—this thing called mercy. In fact, it seems in Ezekiel 16, the more the people strayed from

---

1   Robert Frost. "Fire and Ice." Retrieved from https://www.poetryfoundation.org/poems/44263/fire-and-ice.

God, the more determined God became to restore them, to remember his covenant with them. And we say that beautiful psalm of repentance in this Lenten season: "Cleanse me of sin with hyssop, that I may be purified; wash me, and I shall be whiter than snow" (51:9).

The world may end, with fire or ice, but God's mercy, the Psalmist says, is everlasting (e.g. Ps. 103:8; Ps. 118:1-4).

This should have been crystal clear to those who come to this communion table. Though our sins be as scarlet, we are welcome here. We just have to hunger and thirst for him, and we will find our icy hearts melting and our cold hands reaching out to help warm others. For, on the night before he died, he took bread…

A Communion Meditation

So we have this little house on the Allegheny River in Pennsylvania. In the backyard is a little flower garden. In the middle of it, I planted a metal pole (see if you can eat that, you deer!). On top of it, I installed a bird house with an entrance hole just big enough for a wren or a chickadee. Soon a male House Wren began building a nest in it while calling every few minutes to see if he could attract a mate. He did. In researching wrens, I found out that the male starts the nest and if she likes it, she finishes it, rearranging it to her liking—are we descended from wrens or what? We watched those parents go in and out of that house for weeks. Then they started bringing food in and sometimes taking the garbage (like egg shells) out.

One day weeks later, while my daughter and son-in-law were watching, we saw a head appear at the opening, look around, hesitate, and then take its first wobbly flight to a nearby bush. Then another came out and another. One clung to the opening, but the next one pushed him or her so he had no choice but to fly. I think I counted seven baby wrens who flew from that little house, like clowns from a Volkswagen!

Think of it: They went from being taken care of totally, being wing to wing in crowded quarters with their brothers and sisters, to a completely new form of existence. But it was as if they were always being prepared for their first flight, for having to find their own food, escape their predators, and eventually build their own nests.

It struck me that this might be a metaphor for our Christian lives. We Christians believe that we are taken care of by a loving God. We are fed at this table. Then we are sent out into the world to live a life that may be completely foreign and strange—because it's a life that follows our leader in non-violent support for the poor, the suffering, and the oppressed, a life that takes care of the earth and tries to make community happen—a life we never realized we were being prepared for. We grow too big for the birdhouse. We are challenged to fly.

I've never seen parent wrens feed their young after they are fledged. But we have a God who doesn't abandon us, who cares for us, and feeds us here. And we are in turn moved to feed and support each other through the difficult and often scary flights through life.

For, on the night before he died, he took bread....

It Is Finished–Good Friday 2015[1]

I had the privilege, the honor and the great sadness of being present at the deaths of both my mother and father. They did not die in a hospital or suddenly. They died at home, in bed. I suppose it is a common inclination to dwell on their last words.   We remember last words. My three siblings and I have agreed that Dad's last words were: "Get some rest." He apparently felt we were taxing ourselves hovering around his bed. And my mother's? The ones I remember the best as she spent her nine last days in a semi-comatose state were: "Take time to smell the roses!"

And so there are these three last words of Jesus: "It is finished!" They are only recorded in John's Gospel. John was reportedly at the foot of the cross; he would certainly remember them. Or perhaps he wanted these words to sum up the story of Jesus, who was John's hero, the person he equated with the Word, with God, and wasn't John the disciple Jesus loved?

So what did Jesus mean when he cried out: "It is finished?" What does the "IT" refer to? The words are translated in Latin as Consummatum est ["It is consummated!"] But look at the original Greek: The word is tetelestai which was written on business receipts in New Testament times indicating that a bill had been paid in full.

And so to John's Greek-speaking readership; it would be unmistakable that Jesus Christ had died to pay for their sins. [From: Bible.org].

So that's the usual interpretation: And if we agree with it, if we feel we are now close to understanding who God is, if we feel that we owe it to hundreds of years of tradition to believe that Jesus was the scapegoat for our sins, we will feel—what? Guilty?, Repentant? –but comforted? grateful? We laid our sins on him and he was killed so that God could once again love us or see only the sacrifice of his son instead of our ugly sins.

---

1   Presented at St. Paul's Episcopal Church, Cleveland Heights, Ohio on Good Friday, April 3, 2015. Also, Jeannine LaGuardia Joseph, Joe's daughter, read portions of this piece at Joe's memorial service.

It is almost completely irresistible to accept this interpretation. "It is finished" then means that our sins were paid for; God's wrath appeased; we are redeemed, bought back, restored by the Second Adam to the favor that the first Adam (and his wife, of course) screwed up, lost, forfeited—the original sin!

It is comforting, isn't it, to trace Scripture from that fateful third book of Genesis through the Exodus and Law and Judges and Kings and Prophets and Gospels and Letters and Revelation to conclude: Jesus was sent by God to sacrifice himself for our sins, to save us from God's wrath and from hell.   And when he died, It Was Finished! He had saved us; he had redeemed us, bought us back with his blood, appeased his Father, took away our sins! Isn't that what we believe (John 3:16) and what our beloved hymns proclaim and perhaps why we are here during these three hours today, on Good Friday?

May I turn this jewel of Good Friday slightly to consider it from a different angle? Doesn't that traditional interpretation create the danger of freeing us from paying very close attention to Jesus's LIFE? –A life so concerned with the people at society's margins: the poor, the diseased, the possessed, the despised tax collectors and sinners, the aliens (we would call them immigrants now, wouldn't we?), people of low status in those days like children and widows and prostitutes and thieves; and now if we are concerned with where to find him since his body ascended into heaven?: ah yes, says Matthew 25, we find him in the hungry and thirsty and naked and imprisoned.

Pope Francis couldn't resist putting a Latin phrase into his Lenten sermon this year: "Fac cor nostrum secundum cor tuum," meaning "Make our hearts like yours." Does it make any sense to interpret "It is finished" as Jesus saying: "My life is my example for you humans that I love. I did not consider being equal to God a thing to be clung to, but emptied myself and took the form of a servant (Phillipians 2). IF you follow my example, I will have SAVED you. My example of praying, doing and acting; relying on my Father for help and support, will make it possible for you to get beyond your selfishness, even your irritation and hatred of each other and to love my father with all your hearts, and to love each other as you wish to be loved."

The question is phrased—perhaps irreverently—by Tony Jones in his new book: Did God kill Jesus?. No. God so loved the word, He sent His Son to show us the Way to save us from ourselves; and so that, writes Jones, God could experience suffering and dying and violence and even–abandonment. In becoming human, writes Jones, God learned about, FELT, our suffering, our dying, and our feelings of abandonment that He/She could not experience as God!

That was the plan. That IS the plan. And it's all about love, about God being with us. –Difficult love in a cracked world. As Chittister once said,

> *God didn't make nuclear weapons; WE did! And we can unmake them as soon as we WANT to!" But what would it take to want to unmake them? "Did you not suppose," the evangelist Matthew (26:53) quoted Jesus when the powers-that-were came to arrest him, "that I can call on my Father to provide in a moment's notice more than twelve legions of angels?[1]*

What would it take for us NOT to counter violence with violence? –to make our hearts like his? Violence stopped with him. The world was so cracked that people in it killed Jesus rather than have their structures of oppression overturned. They couldn't stand it that a LOT of people wanted to be like him, follow him, to be led by that kind of King.

We have a long way to go. The turning around, the metanoia necessary for us to—as Brian McLaren quoted on the cover of his book—"make the road by walking"[2] is not as easy as doing an about face like a marine at the tomb of the unknown soldier. After all, the people closest to Jesus didn't get it either; they completely missed what he was meaning. Some say he spoke in parables so they would have to think about them and not immediately accept or reject his ideas .

---

1 Chittister, TEDTalk.
2 Brian McLaren. *We Make the Road by Walking.* (Nashville: Jericho Books, 2015).

The kingdom of heaven is like a woman who lost a coin, a shepherd who lost a sheep, a man who fell among thieves, a son who ran off with his inheritance. A lot to think about, because it's a completely DIFFERENT notion of what a kingdom is! Riding into Jerusalem on a donkey was NOT about humility, but about leadership, kingship. Kings at that time did this at their annual enthronement celebrations: they rode into the city on a donkey. But shortly after his procession, at the Passover meal, Jesus washed his disciples' feet. "Here's the kind of King I am. Here's the paradigm to follow. It will bring you suffering, if you continue after I finish. And I have to finish my bodily experience here so I can become your cosmic Christ, your way through suffering, so I can send you my Spirit!"

My father's last words –"Get some rest," come back to me when I have at last put some meditation time into my daily schedule and when I see all of the wonderful emphases these days on contemplation by people like Richard Rohr, and eastern mysticism by people like the Buddhist nun, Ani Palmo, and the prayer groups all over the place. "Get some rest" now means to me: Experience the presence of God! And my Mother's admonition to take time to smell the roses now reminds me of Taylor's *Altar of the World* and Brueggeman's book on the Sabbath, Henri Nouwen's hands open to new realities, Thich Nhat Hanh's contemplative prayer, and my dear Rev. Cam Miller, an episcopal priest who moved from Buffalo to a town in rural Vermont, but who writes a blog that is read by people all over the world. And then there's Nadia Bolz-Weber, Rachel Held Evans, Sarah Bessey, and yes, Marcus Borg.

Marcus Borg died on January 21, 2015 at the age of 72. His memorial service at Trinity Episcopal in Portland, Oregon was just held this past Sunday. You may have heard him speak during one of his trips to Cleveland. He wrote over 20 books, but the one just published certainly contains HIS LAST words. It's called Convictions. It will lead you to a new approach to Scripture and to a whole new understanding of Jesus's words. I wish I had time to summarize Borg's words for you. Join any group that studies it.

Neither my mother nor my father (nor Jesus, I think) would want me to spend the rest of my days getting some rest and smelling roses. No. Before I am finished, I need to make the road by walking, to hear the cries of the people, to show up every day and do what I can, to practice what I preach. We have each other. You at St. Paul's and we at Heights Christian and so many other congregations represented here, are examples of people doing things for others, having a care for this earth ("Look at those lilies," Jesus said. "LOOK at them!" with the same awe that our four year old granddaughter lavished on her first sight of a full-blooming amaryllis that we gave her as a bulb for Christmas). I know you are members of the Greater Cleveland Congregations that are non-violently making things happen within the structures of our society, just as Jesus did. And we at Heights Christian, continuing the feistiness and pizzazz of our forefathers and mothers who built our church during the Great Depression, have summed up our mission statement in just two words: "Building community!"

Our work is by no means finished. We are finishing what He started. And we stand here today so grateful that 2000 plus years ago, a Jewish man possibly in his early 30s summed up all he had said and done as the Eternal Word in human form in these wonderful last words: "It is finished!"

And when it comes time for us to say "it is finished" because we are dying, we can be so grateful to God and Jesus. We can say "You did such a good thing, because now you know what it is like to suffer and die; you are with us. You have taught us we can let go; we can get through this. There is another side. There is light; there may be lilies, and we will look at them in wonder and love." Amen.

Poetry

Cameo

I cannot have this world

Just for myself

For everywhere I go

I find the leavings

Of some prior lessor of the land;

So maybe if I choose a scene

And frame it like a picture-taker does,

I'll keep it safely cameoed

In the album of my heart.

God Must Be Like That

God must be like that:

She picks you out of a crowd

Who hardly know your name,

And turns her face to you

With eyes that long ago

Put judgment in a box

And now forgets just where

She laid the key.

She smiles and says some words

Of thanks or praise.

You feel as if you've had a drink

Of water, mountain-clear and cool,

And so you find your way again

–Refreshed—

And hurry on,

Remembering those moments of her gaze

When you were touched

By joy.

Micah's Daughter

In honor of Sr. Rosemary Hocevar, OSU

*"..And what does the Lord require of you but to do justice, and
to love kindness, and to walk humbly with your God?"*
(Micah 6:8)

Time is not the essence

When your very name

Is one of the other herbs

And all your time was spent

Adding zest to life

And fighting for the young

Who did not have the pungency

To craft a better life…

You walked on Micah's words

As if they were the stepping stones

Across that vast and watery expanse

Called "Education."

We see you there still beckoning

To those of us who fear

For crocodiles and drowning:

"Just hold my hand," you say,

"And plant your feet

On these my stones."

And so we do, with faith

That even if this darkling fog

Prevents our seeing you,

The memory of that beckoning hand

And eager voice

Will force our following.

On a Minister's Leaving

For Jayne Kuroiwa

Our holy Master long ago

Compared his words to seeds…

Our granaries are full of them

Both his and ours (and yours).

And yours unpublished vanished

As soon as they were said

Like bubbles exquisite

And crystal clear and colorful and brief.

At least, I thought they did

Until I took a closer look at this old soil

And found some sprouts like memories

Enlivening my soul

And others, too, a field of soft green shoots

That have us thinking now

Of growth and cultivation.

These Four

In remembrance of Dr. Ginny Marion

If Goodness could encapsulate itself

And hide like summer sun does

In garden fresh tomatoes

If Courage could reveal its shape

Like autumn leaves

Strip tease their colors

If Joy could find a nest for winter

And stock it

Full of nuts

If Wisdom could arrive without a limp

And curl up before

A crackling fire

Then we would recognize these four

Already showed themselves to us

And glisten in our memories.

You Have Been a Light (1 John 1:7)

You have been a light here,

People feel it like the warmth of sun on skin,

Sometimes casting shadows like an Ansel Adam's photo

So that what before seemed unremarkable

Now stands appreciated and alive.

The word repeats two hundred fifty times and more

In Sacred Scripture,

Shining through the holy text

As if the God behind it wanted us to blink

At dazzling glimpses coming through the message of those words,

Enticing us to grasp what is behind and underneath

And is to come.

You've walked within the power and protection of that light,

Reflecting in your ministry the countless colors hidden and refracted there.

They say that some go trailing light

Leaving it behind as sparks and embers which, if tended well,

Will burn anew and transfer warmth to future travelers.

You have been and shared a light

And John of old knew what to call it:

Love.

Of Immense Significance–
First Floor Men's Room

Seeing where the holes

In a bathroom floor were plugged–

The nubs in the ceramic tile

Where the anchors to the private stall had set–

Before the room itself became secure

And now is locked when only one inhabitant

Rushes in to this most intimate of space–

Reminded me that I remembered

Where the Robin built its nest this year,

And how the lines around your eyes

Gather up to frame your sparkling face…

So that I nearly stumbled when these proofs

Collided to convince me

Of my oneness with all things.

The Search

I am searching for a metaphor

To symbolize this ache

So I can put it in a mortar

And grind away at it

Until it gets so light

A breeze will scatter it

And I can think it stardust

To be flung

In total desolation

At the moon.

Why? A Christmas Poem 2013

The fountain stands quite frozen now

The waters of the lake are still.

The trees that still have limbs

Are now denuded of their leaves.

And artificial lights inside

Are not quite able to inspire

Beyond an artificial joy.

Yet Christmas break has sent our students home

And lays a challenge at the door

Of freezing tissue in our hearts and minds:

Who is this God whose birth we honor

And why on earth would He or She

Decide to join in our impermanence?

But then we start to count the kindnesses

The cookies, smiles and gifts,

The invitations to our tables and our plans;

We see a smiling Pope

Whose hat was nearly knocked askew

By the lad who filled his arms,

This Pope whose words keep urging us

To love and heal and always hope.

And then—by Gosh!–we feel God here

Peeking, as we did when three or four,

Beneath the wrappings and the coverlets

To find the Gifts we now acknowledge were

Just tokens smeared with love, and so

We start to understand Emmanuel

And why.

Flirting God

I see you,

Peeking out at me

From that foreboding cloud…

And, by the way,

That perfume is not fair

Especially since you change it every day

And now you smell like autumn leaves

And misty air.

And do not blink at me

Through limbs that throw their shadows on my wall

(However will my work get done?)

Or whisper in such husky tones

Before you say goodnight

And lay your fingers lightly on my eyes.

Have you not researched my life?

And therefore know I'm hardly nice to be around?

How can you claim me as your friend,

And look at me in silence with those starry eyes?

Stop tempting me to fall in love with you!

You know I've failed your every test!

My wickedness gets scorched to ashes

In the noontime of your focused lens

My cherished fears are all escaping from my grasp,

And now I'm looking forward to that leap into your arms!

So catch me, if you can!

Prayers

Numbering Our Days Alright

Lord, we come before you this morning knowing there is so much we do not understand   We don't understand how time can go so fast when we count up birthdays and anniversaries and the age of children and grandchildren. But then how can time progress so slowly when we are worried, or ill, or in pain?

And so we pray with the psalmist: "Teach us to number our days aright." Moreover, teach us just how to be, how to be in the present moment and how to let go of all the stuff that drags us back into the past or makes us afraid of the future. Show us how to give you time, maybe just in ten-second intervals, several times a day, shutting down our thoughts and fears. We can do it. For ten seconds, starting now: nine eight seven six five four three two one.

And then refreshed and renewed, we can bring you our prayers for all the people and situations that need them as we pray: "Lord, in your mercy, hear our prayer."

Prayer for Worship

Lord, we are here

We may be only partially here

Because our minds are taken up

With problems and worries.

We are like spring in this city

Daring to peek through the soil

Fearing we may be frozen

But we are here

Trying to listen to your Word

Our hearts thawing

Open to Communion

Ready to pray

Eager to worship you, our God and Creator,

Our eternal springtime.

Autumn Prayer

Dear God,

As we experience the cycles of life, we use metaphors to help us cope and understand. And so we talk about pendulums swinging from one extreme to another; and about things going around and coming around full circle. And now we are challenged by something that is not a metaphor, but is a season. Seasons come and seasons go, we say. What are you teaching us, Lord, through these beautiful colors, through the death of leaves and their flutter to the ground to become the humus for next season's spring? Are you encouraging us to wait in hope through down times and bad weather? Are you reminding us that the tilt of our planet does not mean the sun's warmth has gone forever? Are you giving us this time and this sign to allow ourselves to get a little emptier, to let a little more of our true spirit show through the chlorophyll of our exterior persona, to let others warm us in this chill as we do for them? Teach us autumn lessons, Lord, we pray. Amen.

On the Edge of Autumn

Season of greenfulness,

Riding on a blue planet

As it slowly tips away from the sun

And causes your green leaves

To undress themselves in the chemistry of fall

And show the colors hiding under chlorophyll.

Dear God, we wear our images so long and carefully,

As if to hide our true colors

From the embarrassing light of day;

And so we ask you—poised on the edge of fall

To let us tip our hearts closer to you

And let you deal with all our shame.

Your son forgave his murderers;

We know he will forgive us, too

(Do we even have to ask?)

So that we can cover others' shame and hurt

With the colors of compassion

And so we pray: "Lord, in your mercy, hear our prayer."

*****

The weight of our pain and fear can overwhelm us, Lord;

We need you to flex your strong arms

And gently lift these burdens from us all

Then we will rest in you like autumn leaves on warm October ground,

And catalog and lend your colors to a weary world.

We start right now by praying: "Our Father…"

Snowflake Prayer

O God,

They say that no two snowflakes are alike. So here we are—like snow-flakes—no two of us alike. And all of us have fallen here, today, into this time and place. Although we have our own unique structure, quite nice, and frozen in us by genes and family and culture and education, we might, like snow, be most alluring when we join ourselves to some common effort—like transforming the ugliness that we often encounter before the world is beautified by our soft touch.

Snowflakes are just a metaphor, we know, but then there are the people who have gone before us and have looked to you for guidance and shaped their lives according to your way: those people spoke and wrote that the best thing we can do is melt: by giving our very selves to you and to all those who you likewise love and maybe losing all those edges that prevent us from joining each other in our great work of transformation. Amen.

Spring Prayer 2014

Dear God, in our part of the country, spring comes with a lot of expectations. After a winter like the one just past, we expect spring to be warm, and SUNNY, rejuvenating and beautiful. We want to work the soil and clean the house and get the road salt residue off of our cars. It can be a terrible disappointment to find spring a muddy mess, with dreary days and chilly temperatures and snow still in the forecast.

But we are just the same, aren't we? With all of our gifts and education and contacts, we often stand before you a muddy mess. And so we take great consolation from reading the Scriptures that seem to indicate that you love muddy messes. As a mother embraces a child who comes home bruised and dirty and crying, so you embrace us with all of our rumpled baggage, and give us much hope that the sun will soon peak through the clouds, the crocuses will bloom, the birds build their nests and—bolstered by your creative power—the world will move an inch closer to goodness. This is our prayer, as we join you in that creative endeavor today. Amen.

We Showed Up

Something has brought us to this room today—something besides the entry in our calendars or the email reminding us or the items on the agenda. Something long ago started us on a path that has led to this room. It's been a journey fraught with hardships, unexpected turns, maybe even some painful falls that brought our faces into contact with the dirt of our path.

But we kept on. People lifted us up and supported us. We believed this was the best road for us to travel. We hoped we had something to offer, something unique, something transformative. We may be weary now, but there was once a spark, and it wouldn't take much to remember it and–if needed–rekindle it. It is as ancient as fire, as a Passover to freedom, as a journey from death to life. It smolders at times, sends up pungent fumes at times, but is never extinguished.

So, OK: Someone has brought us to this room today, Someone who is often discovered in fire, and Whose warmth embraces us and those who stand near us. Amen.

New Beginnings Prayer
after Genesis 1-3

Creator God, in calling You Creator, we acknowledge You as the God of our Beginnings, all beginnings.

And so we ask you to bless our beginnings this year. We ask you for light, and to help us separate light from the darkness of ignorance and selfish myopia.

We ask you for the moon and stars, because our dreams are big and our aspirations great.

We ask you to focus our attention on the beauty of this blue and green and brown earth and to protect us from the sharks and killer whales that often seem to lurk as we swim in your ocean of air.

We ask you to help us respect the snakes and crawling things while resisting the temptation to act on their level or to climb up the false tower of our own hubris thinking we are better and taller and more independent of you than we are.

And finally, we ask you to teach us how to get along, to keep us from wanting to kill each other, to show us how to talk politely about our differences and even to celebrate them.

We accept the beginnings you have entrusted to us. We hold them in our hands and wonder at their promise. We promise to take care of them and to return them to you even better than they now are. But for this we need your hand on ours, loving us, consoling us, energizing us, renewing us and keeping us faithful. Amen.

Pastoral Prayer 11-6-16

Dear Father whom we dare to call Ours, we know that election is about choosing.   We have many examples in Scripture of your choosing individuals like Abraham and Joseph and Elijah and Elisha, and Samuel and Solomon, and David, and Joseph and Mary, and Peter and Paul and a whole community called Israel.

So today we ask you to choose us. No. We know from your Son and our Lord Jesus Christ that you have already chosen us. We have come to believe that your Spirit works within and among us. And so I guess we are asking you to re-choose us at this critical time in our nation's history.

You know our needs. You know how we have fought for land as did that first community that you chose. You know how we have deviated from our ideals and have been stingy with our love and have hated our ene-mies. But we are still trying, dear Father, we are still repenting of our past sins. We ask you to forgive us and paint for us once again a picture of the peaceable kingdom that your son can bring about.

And now we lift up our prayers to you, as we say: "Lord, in your mercy, hear our prayer."

****

If the lion and the lamb can and will lie down together, surely we of dif-fering political opinions can co-exist and wish each other well. Commit us to do good, to renew our determination to follow your Son's Way, to follow BOTH of the great commandments, to acknowledge that we are brothers and sisters in Jesus.

Because when we reflect on our history, when we review our blessings, when we remember our purple mountains' majesty, when we see what good is being done by so many people, we are so grateful. We see these things and people as sacraments of you. We know that your Son did not pitch his tent among us to change your mind about us, but to change our mind about you—You who are our dear Lord, and our loving Father.

And so we pray: "Our Father..."

Pastoral Prayer

Dear Lord,

In this part of the country, summer is our chance to take off our shoes and feel the soil,

Perhaps find a patch of grass that has not yet been adulterated with carcinogenic pesticides

We believe in what Hopkins wrote –that the Holy Spirit is like a bird warming the earth, hatching new and wonderful things

Please make us aware of that Spirit, Your Spirit. Come, Holy Spirit, we pray (Veni, Sancte Spiritus!)

We need your Spirit, and we trust that you will NOT leave us orphans

But will continue to inspire us, to join us together in creating, planting

Helping each other to protect and sustain your beautiful creation

Help us to remove whatever prevents us from seeing it, feeling it, loving it

And hear our prayers for those who cannot appreciate it because they are suffering and are in need, and for them we pray:

"Lord, in your mercy hear our prayer."

******

Were it not for your Spirit, your presence, and experiencing you in the people you gather here

We might despair of accomplishing so much with so little

We are like the snails that Zen Masters cheered on to climb Mt. Fuji, but slowly, slowly.

Help us to keep on, slowly offering our prayers and resources, reaching out a hand, giving some of our harvest,

Not letting criticism and cynicism deter nor discourage us, never giving up, always pressing through tiredness and obstacles.

Because you remind us, refresh us, and cajole us with your presence in perfect summer days.   Amen.

Sermons

No Charge for Baggage

I am happy to see all of you here today and I feel privileged to be the "preacher of the day." I think there would have been more people here, but when they saw the sermon title on the marquee, they said: "I know what he's going to say; I've heard it all before, so I think I'll stay home and work in my garden."

Here's what I think THEY think I will say on this topic: That lots of us have lots of baggage, but God doesn't care how much baggage we have. He loves and accepts us. Ok. That IS what I am going to say, but with a whole lot more words (wait! Don't leave!) and I hope a couple different perspectives.

The first thing those travelers up Van Aken need to know is: I'm NOT talking about baggage for the journey into the NEXT life! I'm talking about right here, right now. Here's what Rev. Cam Miller has to say about that:

As far as I am concerned,

and this is just one man's opinion,

way too much about Christianity is invested

in the other side of that choice.

I think it is an enormously profound act of faith

to be engaged in a spiritual practice

that pays no attention

to the other side

until we get there.

Personally,

it seems to me that the primary act of faith

is to trust God with the unknown

and focus on this side

without anxiety about the other side.[1]

First, let's make a distinction between REAL baggage and meta-phorical baggage. I'm embarrassed by both. When I tell my wife I'm just going to our little house in Pennsylvania to cut the grass, I can see her looking at my huge overnight bag, my fishing equipment, my books, my computer, my chargers (can't go anywhere without chargers), my grass cutting accessories, lots of food, my hedge clippers and my chain saw (in case a tree has fallen across the driveway) and you get the idea. I'm sure she is thinking: HOW long are you staying? That kind of baggage is certainly a symptom of the metaphorical or spiritual baggage that this sermon is mostly about (what does it say about me that I can't go anywhere without a book? –or a cell phone?).

Back to spiritual baggage: There's the baggage of the PAST—the things you've done that you feel guilty about and can never forgive yourself for. We can easily paraphrase Psalm 51:3 to read: "The weight of my offenses is before me always."

Then there are the secrets that you are harboring about yourself— the stuff you'd die a thousand deaths if people knew, (but most people see it anyway). Sneak a cigarette, a drink, a subscription to Cosmopoli-tan? Rev. Richard Rohr calls this hidden self our "Shadow Self."

Then there are the annoying character flaws and habits you (after all these years) still carry into your everyday life: maybe the inability to pay attention to your spouse's instructions beyond the first sentence; or your annoying practice of starting to clean the house and wash the dishes before the last guests have departed, giving a clear message that they should have departed an hour ago in your humble opinion; or the way you don't anticipate what someone might need (how about those people who stand and talk in the doorway so that no one else can get into the room?), or the problems you have expressing your feelings, cleaning up <u>after yourself, or te</u>aring yourself away from constant working so that

1   Miller, *The Subversive Preacher*. https://subversivepreacher.org/subver-sivepreaching-sermons-preacher-helps.

you can have a meaningful, intimate conversation with someone—again you get the idea.

There is also the baggage that comes from the way you were raised, from your 'parent tapes,' as one psychologist calls them.

I keep thinking of the rich young man in Matthew's Gospel, a man who had kept all of the commandments (or at least the ones that Jesus quoted for him) all his life, and who had everything money could buy, and yet he found an empty place, a vacuum, a painful absence: "What else do I lack?" he whimpers to Jesus. "Well, if you want to be perfect," Jesus proclaims, "Go and sell all that you possess and give it to the poor, and come follow me." In other words, get rid of, or at least get detached from, your baggage!

Would one way of detaching from our baggage be to use the gifts that are contained in it for the benefit of others? Does it matter if we get paid for those gifts? For example, suppose I have the gift of music. I'm proud of it. Let's say I'm a concert pianist. It's a gift. I've worked hard to perfect it. I have lots of piano concertos memorized. I'm 27 year old Yuja Wang born in China.

Now how can I give such a gift away? Isn't it a matter of how I approach that gift? Of how I am looking at that piece of baggage from heaven, even when I am on stage playing with an orchestra?   Consider being a member of our choir. It's one thing to be going up those steps in the sanctuary, knowing I look good in my new suit and tie, and knowing my voice will sound good and blend in well, and I know the notes for a change; and IT'S QUITE ANOTHER THING to forget all that and sing as a ministry, as Dale Hukill and Willie Wright challenge us to do, asking God's spirit to sing with and through me. Isn't that to detach from some of my wealth, some of my baggage?

Subtle, I know. Not much difference–or does such an approach make ALL the difference?

Let me tell you the story of Slomo. This is a true story, about a doctor, a neurologist, I think, who had it all, had risen to the top of his profession, lived in a mansion, drove both a 12-cylinder BMW and a Jaguar.   But he felt suffocated by all this baggage! And so when his vision started to go, he resigned, moved into a studio apartment near a beach, and his main task each day was to skate! –in line skate, With his one arm pointing ahead of him and one leg lifted up and pointing behind him. People didn't know who he was. Some thought he was homeless (but with really nice skates). They called him Slomo.   He felt he was simply doing what he wanted to do. But he also found that such skating gave him the feeling of flying. He felt he was both connected with the center of the earth and WITH GOD, free at last.

And there's the reason for dealing with our baggage, this union with God. What can we do with our baggage? Well, some of us may need professional help to deal with it. Others of us can find healing in Eckhart Tolle's admonition NOT to confuse our life situation (with all its baggage) with OUR LIFE, what Rohr calls our "TRUE SELF." Most of us can practice letting go of our baggage by meditating daily, using a mantra as our only word, returning to it whenever our mind wanders. It's a practice of being in silence with no words (and therefore, no baggage).

But how, you ask me, are we ever to transform the world as Jesus commissions if we are dealing with our own and other people's baggage?

I don't know. I DO know that some people are transforming the world by taking in other people's baggage, some of it or all of it, just like God does for us, for NO CHARGE. Here, I think of many of you who are doing just this.   For example, a woman not from this congregation told me recently, she took her son back into her house after he came out of prison, with full knowledge that she didn't know what the future would bring, but with the certainty that she was being called to do this for her son.

Others have used their gifts of understanding and tolerance like a baggage train or carousel at an airport—to assist others in carrying their heavy loads, and maybe to sell or unload some of them. I'm thinking here of the professor we recently interviewed in a Skype call from Israel. She went there to teach Palestinians and Israelis the concept of "peaceful coexistence," which they are now calling "shared life" (because of all the baggage contained in the phrase "peaceful coexistence"). She feels that her work has made a difference if someone who was vehemently focused on his/her own position, moves from that simplicity to the complexity of knowing there might be another way, some common ground. –From simplicity to complexity—who would have named that success?

From the outside looking in, some people's baggage looks like clothes tied into knots or an onion (to add a metaphor) and this baggage can be untied only if they will allow their mind and heart to experience a new insight. For example, as some have written who have moved out of their fundamentalist vision, if you have been interpreting the Bible all your life as a literal expression of God's law, as a how-to book, every word of which is inspired, and now you can realize that the Bible is a collection of books, all written by different people at different times in the world's history, and that each one of them had a culture, a perspective, and a message to communicate. If you can do this, you may have peeled away a layer of baggage.

Unlocking your heart, your pre-judgments, even your religious and political opinions is extremely difficult. It can feel like dying and leave you confused and floundering at first. But it can be a wondrously liberating feeling of getting rid of baggage. "Let's rent a dumpster," I said as I contemplated the state of our basement. Or: As I related in our last Bible study when we were considering that wonderful passage on the Faithful or Valiant Woman in the book of Proverbs (chapter 31), it is so wonderful and liberating to realize that that chapter of Proverbs is a poem. It is a poem TO women, NOT a proscription to make women feel guilty as it is trotted out and read in churches on Mother's Day, or applied to some valiant mother who has died, making every other female in the congregation wonder how THEY are measuring up!

But it turns out that this sermon title is only partly true. This IS a charge for baggage, an exorbitant charge, a terrible charge. The baggage we carry from our past abuse, sins, unkindness, jealousy, revenge, short sightedness and a ton else has been carried with us. The rich young man in the Gospel felt it as a great hole in his heart: What do I lack? This baggage has weighed us down and poisoned relationships. It has been suppressed so that we can tolerate ourselves, but that suppression is known by every psychologist to cause myriads of problems—like a volcano that keeps building pressure until it finally spews destructive smoke and ash and fire.

And the thing is, the wonderful thing, the price of admission, the gift of faith and hope is: God uses our baggage as if it were a gigantic plot in a love story. God uses it to curb our arrogance, encourage us to reach out and say: "To whom shall we go? You have the words of [eternal] life!" Our baggage turns out to be the stones that enable us to hop across the raging stream of life into the loving arms of God. "You mean You PLANNED all of this?" we might ask God. "Well," he might say, "Let's just say I used it to get you to me."

Can you imagine a God, who, with a twinkle in his eye and an upturned mouth, welcomes you and your pile of suitcases filled with baggage, saying: "Come to me, you who are weary and heavy laden , and I will give you rest! Take my yoke upon you and learn from me, for I am gentle and humble of heart, and you will find rest for your souls. For my yoke is easy and my burden is light" (Mt. 11:28-30). That is, take my baggage. It is light and it will make you feel wonderful to carry it! Without him, we can do nothing and with him, we can do all things (As Paul writes in Phillipians 4:13 "I can do all things in him who strengthens me"). God wants to heal us NOW.

I'll bet the people zipping past this sermon title in our front lawn had no idea that it would be reduced to a number of paradoxes: if you have baggage, let it go or let God carry it; if you don't have so much baggage, look to help someone else carry theirs. God has carried everyone's and we may be called to help him with it. Some people have shoulders, spirits that big…

So here's the sign posted by God at the doorway to a deeper spiritual life.

No charge for baggage; if you haven't been able to let it go, I want you to let me carry it:

Your hurts or wounds from the past

Your guilt

Your sins and addictions

Your relationship baggage between spouses, parents, and other relatives

Your wealth

Your fears and worries.

"Come, all you who labor and are burdened, and I shall give you rest." We can say Amen to that, right?

But now, God says, I expect you to carry MINE.

When the Door Is Barred

Life can be full of annoyances. Back in the day before cell phones and smart phones when important people always carried a beeper, one of those important men (he was a scientist from NASA) was standing in a checkout line in the grocery store. A mother and her young boy were standing behind him. All of a sudden his beeper went off, and the little boy cried out: "Watch out, mommy, that fat man is backing up!"

Ever since the spring, there has been construction work going on at the church across the street from our house, and promptly at 7 a.m., a fat little, green little cherry picker would make this piercing sound when it went either up or down, forwards or backwards, [now why does it need to beep when it goes up in the air? Is it warning low-flying birds?]. My wife and I for the first time in our lives, wished for a bazooka or a rocket launcher to disable that screaming contraption.

When I looked at the lectionary to find out what the readings were for today, it turned out that—although this is what is called "Ordinary Time" in the church year, the 22nd Sunday after Pentecost—there were eight different choices for readings! How annoying is that?

And One of them, from the book of Amos, a minor Prophet, reminded me unnecessarily that there is more to life than the minor annoyances that irritate you so badly as you are growing older and conspire to turn you inwards so that you become crabbed and crabby, a truly miserable person (like that little green cherry picker). Amos talks about the "day of the Lord," and prophesies that "It will be darkness and not light; As when a man flees from a lion and a bear meets him, Or goes home, leans his hand against the wall and a snake bites him" (Amos 5: 18b-19). Now these are life-changing annoyances!

They remind us unnecessarily that the world is a cracked and scary place, even without us in it, we who are often plotting to do evil instead of good! The spiritual person, the person who prays—wonderfully or badly—learns to say YES to this cracked and scary place, to do as Jesus did—in the manger and on the cross: to hold, even embrace, the nonsensicalness of our existence, the beauty and the ugliness, the awesomeness plus the natural disasters, the terrible mistakes and the downright, deliberate evil-doing. One such person is Ann Voskamp, who made it her goal to write down 1,000 things she was thankful for, which she published in her book One Thousand Gifts.

In a few short weeks, we will be entering the season of Advent. We are not waiting for Jesus to be born. That's already happened. But we may be waiting to grasp what we believe about that birth and the consequences of it. "Have this mind in you," Paul sings in his letter to the Philippians. God entered our miserable, wonderful, often annoying, existence. He looked into the face of a Mother and Father who loved him to pieces, but he had to put up with the smell of sheep and donkeys, the cold nights and sweltering days in the desert, and all the annoyances of growing into adulthood in a time that had none of the conveniences that we today cannot do without.

And when he was an adult, he told this story which was remembered, and written down by Matthew. He told many stories like this, a parable meant to be pondered and unpacked for its many meanings:

There were five wise virgins or bridesmaids and five foolish. Their mission is to escort the bridegroom to the house of the bride and then escort both to the place of the wedding and the subsequent feast. The traditional interpretation of the passage has to do with the Second Coming, the Parousia, to hold us all in fear and faithfulness because "he will come like a thief in the night" and we'd better be ready or be sorry for all eternity. But don't we have enough to accept and be afraid of? Allow me to suggest another interpretation in the light of much contemporary spiritual writing.

Two things disturb me about this story: 1. The foolish ones weren't evil or criminal; they just hadn't thought ahead. They made the unwarranted assumptions that the bridegroom would be on time and that there was oil in their lamps. They thought they had enough oil (Levine: oil is a metaphor for righteousness).   How many of us grab our cell phone on the way out the door but neglect to see if its battery is low? Then when the five called foolish asked the wise ones for a little help (I mean oil), the wise ones said NO! –not your typical Christian response! Was that supposed to be tough love? They needed our choir behind them, singing vigorously: "Give me oil for my lamp, keep me burning. Give me oil in my lamp, I pray."

Side comment for another sermon: [Maybe this "NO" is a warning that if we constantly close ourselves off—from people, from new things, from learning, from the whispers and inspirations of God—we will be closed so tight that no one can get any oil, any righteousness, any forgiveness or compassion INTO us!]. But back to the parable:

2. Second disturbing thing, when the foolish ones went to the oil merchants and bought some and came back to the wedding (note: they didn't just give up and go home), they made a second bad assumption: they assumed they'd be let into the feast! But the door was barred, and when they knocked, the master himself took time from his dancing and came out to lecture them about who gets admission, and everyone had better stay alert, because "you know not the day nor the hour." Harsh. No wonder Rev. Cam Miller advised his fellow priests recently to preach AGAINST Matthew at times.

This is not what Jesus does. He may say irritable or harsh words to someone—like the Syrophoenician woman whose daughter was possessed (I'm not casting my bread to the dogs), but then Jesus relents and cures her! Isn't this the Jesus who tells another story about Yet, still, the world is cracked and bad things, terrible things, keep happening.

Bad things come in threes, we are likely to say. So I only had two parents, and I watched each of them die. So where's the third? Was it the death of my wife's sister, or more recently, of my friend and classmate, Fr. Bill Wiethorn? I found out he was sick from my son in law's uncle. Bill wasn't allowed visitors, but the hospital put me through to his ICU bedside. He told me he had pneumonia and inoperable cancer. I said I'd pray for him, but he asked me to "talk to God in my own words." This from a man in a religion that has a prayer book for everything, like a Book of Common Prayer. There are rituals and blessings, words for marriages and funerals. Everything can be read from a book. But here was my friend, in the last days of his life, almost validating MY life by saying: "Talk to God in your own words." Be yourself, that says to me. God loves you. You don't have to get it right by mouthing someone else's approved prayers. Yours are good, sufficient, marvelous, acceptable, loved. Just talk to him.

It's what I want to say to those foolish virgins. You are on the right track. You are following the bridegroom. Sit in the dust before his door and wait for him. Then talk to him in your own words. From the wise virgins the righteous among us learn to stay righteous; when God calls you to do something, you will be ready. But for the rest of us: those who are not so righteous, who are not beyond forgetting our oil or dumping it all over our wedding suits, the foolish virgins are teachers. Here's what they can teach us:

1. When God calls, go right away. Take whatever oil you have; come as you are (I know there is another story about the man who got thrown out of the wedding because he was not dressed appropriately, but these virgins are dressed for a wedding! [Matthew 22]).

2. If no one will help you when you prove inadequate for the task, seek help from those who have been there done that—like the people right here in this community. We can be a support group for each other, or we can start one if needed (as Dahlia is trying to do for single parents). I read another version of the starfish story in Dr. Tatum: a Crowd gathers and they ALL pitch in so that by the end, there are NO starfish dying on the beach! This is what Malala did, and Karen Armstrong, and those many who do TED and TEDx Talks—Ideas worth sharing!

3. Then return to do the work of the Lord—which always comes down to love and compassion (1st and 2nd greatest commandments) or to Micah's words: "Do the right; love goodness, and walk humbly with your God" (6:8).

4. If the door is barred—this is important because a LOT of the great mystics, saints, contemplatives and really holy people have attested to this—if God disappears on you; if the bad news you hear and see every day on TV overwhelms you; if you get so depressed you can hardly get out of bed; if your prayers seem unanswered and tragedy and chaos dogs your days—if, in the words of the parable, you are not getting in for the feast and the bridegroom is not coming out except to load you with guilt, then sit down and wait.

5. To my way of thinking, sitting and waiting means waiting on the Lord, keeping on keeping on as they way, staying with the meditation you are practicing, the volunteering you are doing, the food you are delivering, the chicken soup! the listening to others whose oil is depleted or gone.   As we read in Psalm 27:14: "Wait for the Lord with courage; Be stouthearted and wait for the Lord!" Or hear in one translation of the prophet Isaiah (40:31) these words: "they who wait for the Lord shall renew their strength; they shall mount up with wings like eagles; they shall run and not be weary; they shall walk and not faint."

This world is flawed. It has lots of occasions for pain and heartbreak. If it were perfect, none of us would have reason to figure out what to do, to figure out how to cope, to offer sympathy and empathy, to bring dinners to the sick, to go to wakes and offer condolences, to wait for healing and numbing of wounds too great to bear in the present, to open up our arms and hug and kiss someone in despair.

This waiting is NOT passive, like sitting around in a bar or a football stadium waiting for something interesting to happen. No. It is a saying YES to everything that IS happening—from beepers to impolite drivers, and standing up to assist when we are inspired, prompted, moved, invited to do so.

As one contemporary writer encourages us: "The only people who pray well are those who keep praying. In the dark night, when all other practices and beliefs about God lose their meaning, keep returning to silent, contemplative prayer. It will keep you empty and ready for God's ongoing revelation of an ever deeper love." Translation: you'll have room and be ready for the OIL.[1]

As we anticipate Advent, I close with the words of Rev. Cam Miller:

"New Creation?" we scorn.

"Where is this new creation

and what good has it done?"

"Wait! Wait!" the midwife urges.

"The cervix has thinned and opened

and even now,

even right this minute,

God's new creation is being born.

Don't walk away.

Don't give up.

Don't close your mind now

when we're so close."

And that is when someone

with a wise and patient faith

will see.

That is when someone

with a wise and patient faith

will know

where to look.

The New Creation

is being birthed,

it is not here yet in any kind of fullness,

but the promise

is that it has begun…somehow.

---

1   Rohr. "Daily Meditation," October 15, 2014.

If all we expect to see when we look

is the apocalypse around us

then that is all we will see.

But if we have a notion,

an inkling

that something else

has started,

even now,

we may have the eyes

to perceive it

and…

and become a midwife too.

I think that is what this is all about.

Are we prepared to be a midwife?

Are we prepared to assist God

in her labor?[2]

Let us pray.

Dear God, we come here as often as we can because we believe; we have hope that you are constantly plotting good, no matter what we are plotting. We come here to throw ourselves into the river of your plans, the good things you have set into motion. And if we can't find you today, we come here to wait, and we pray with the psalmist:

I believe that I shall look upon the goodness of the Lord in the land of the living (Ps. 27:13)

Our soul waits for the Lord; he is our help and our shield. For our heart is glad in him, because we trust in his holy name. Let your steadfast love, O Lord, be upon us, even as we hope in you (Ps.33: 20-22).

---

2   Miller, *The Subversive Preacher*, https://subversivepreacher.org/subversivepreaching-sermons-preacher-helps.

For we know that "The Lord is good to those who wait for him, to the soul who seeks him" (Lamentations 3:25).

"For toward you, O God, my Lord, my eyes are turned; in you I take refuge; strip me not of life" (Ps. 141:8).

For Lord, to whom shall we go? In whom shall we put our trust? You have the words of everlasting life!

AMEN!

Stranded

I am gratified and amazed that so many of you made it to church this morning. It reminds me that it is all of us who make a worship service, not just the preacher. This morning, since Joan is stranded, I thought we'd reflect for a few minutes on what it means to be stranded. There are all kinds of being stranded, of course: some physical and many emotional. I can think of places I would NOT want to be stranded in-like in that cave we visited where the tour guide thought it would be cute to turn the lights off so we tourists could experience pitch blackness.

But then there are other types of being stranded: stuck with too many birthdays is one, especially when our bodies don't work as well as they used to and our wives or significant others keep reminding us of what age we are NOT (You are no longer 25!). Some people are stranded in depression, in abusive relationships, in piles of bills that bury them just as surely as avalanches have buried those poor people in Afghanistan. Then there is health and all of the usual downers that we experience in this bent and flawed existence.

Finally, there's the stranded feeling we get when we are called upon to the presiding elder or to stand up and make a speech. Some people call it writer's block, but it can be downright embarrassing when someone reaches out to you for help, wants and needs desperately your words of wisdom, like a son or daughter going off to war, or someone you love gets very sick or is even dying, and you look inside after years of prayer and attending church and reading the bible, and there is nothing there. All your wisdom seems like platitudes, your memorized Bible verses come across as just that—memorized verses to be dragged out at certain times and seasons. But who are you, really? How do you get out of those terrible valleys of being stranded?

As an educational administrator, I was sometimes present when someone was told they would NOT be getting a contract next year. The person often took it quite well. He or She said something about it's being God's will and that there is a plan for everything. And then I remem-

bered our pastor's sermon (was that last week?): What if there IS no
Plan? And his wonderful segue: What if all there is, is LOVE?

Indeed. Some of the greatest mystics wouldn't understand a question like: Does God exist? They KNOW God exists. Why? –Because at
least once in their lives they have had an experience of God. And they
remember it. It didn't solve any of their problems, but they know God
is here, and they have experienced his embrace. Like a soldier on the
front lines, looking at a picture of his mother, his father, his wife or his
girlfriend, the soldier knows they are waiting for him, present to him,
thinking about him every day, longing to embrace him again.

And the same with God.

The worst place to be stranded, of course, according to some contemporary religious thinking, is in HELL. We are going to talk about it
in Bible study today. I even brought a recording by Father Richard Rohr
entitled "Hell, No!" I have been reading Marcus Borg's last book (he
died a couple of weeks ago): Convictions, a big part of which is dedicated to how to interpret Scripture and is a very personal account of how
he came to change his image of God and to come to know Jesus in a
new and different way from merely accepting what he was taught in his
youth. I highly recommend it, because some of us can get stranded in
Scripture.

We used to pray this strange prayer in my own youth: or at least
one line of it now strikes me as strange. I think it was in a formulation
of the Creed, a gathering of all that theologians and church councils
had hammered out over the ages.   I think it was called "The Apostles
Creed." It went something like: Jesus suffered under Pontius Pilate. He
was crucified, died and was buried. He descended into hell, and on the
third day he rose again from the dead. He ascended into heaven and sits
on the right hand of God, the Father Almighty, whence he shall come to
judge the living and the dead."

What on earth could it mean that he descended into hell? Did you
know that hell is not mentioned in the Pentateuch? The Hebrew Scrip-

tures do mention Sheol, a place where you went when you died. But everyone went there, in their thinking. The creed implies that Jesus went there, too, after He died, and then a strong belief has it that he FREED all those who were there.

Otherwise, if we persist is wanting a concept called hell, we have serious problems with Jesus' words about loving enemies, forgiving seventy times seven. In other words, he gives us HOPE that we will NOT be stranded there or anywhere, but in his arms.

We have a LOT to unlearn about God and religion, don't we? We are stranded in so many of our concepts that we should have moved beyond. We have grabbed onto them so fiercely that anyone looking at us would see clenched fists and not open hands.

Henri Nouwen has a book entitled *With Open Hands*, and that's the posture we can try to keep when we feel stranded. As I've told many people, my meditation time has become very simple. It is usually not very effective, in my estimation—and I'm sure some of you, whom I've come to know as great pray-ers, are far beyond me. I visualize a ladder and I descend it step by step, each rung a number from ten to one. When I get to the bottom, I go to a patch of sunlight and just turn my face up to it, relax and try to open myself to its rays. For me, that light is divine, warm, loving.   Darkness does not overcome it, although it tries, as my sins and distractions try to intrude.

That, I think, is a posture for overcoming being stranded. You can imagine mountains in the distance, or a lake before you, and the words of the psalmist will come flooding in: "I lift up my eyes to the mountains. Whence shall help come to me? My help is from the Lord, who made heaven and earth."

This morning, the very few Italian words I know were floating on a melody in my mind from Verdi's opera La Boheme.   They were a gift to help me cope with this new snow. Like Barbara Brown Taylor's words, they were an altar in the world, and a message to wherever I am stranded. "That first kiss of the sun is mine!"[3]

3   Taylor, 52.

Those who ate lunch with us yesterday didn't need a sermon today. There is no place on earth worse to be stranded in than in prison, and we were served by former prisoners at Edwin's Restaurant on Shaker Square yesterday. Brandon, the president, CEO or whatever his title is, addressed us and told us a story that we can easily translate as a tale of someone who paid it forward, walked the talk, acted the Christian way by figuring out how to use his talents to rescue the stranded and give them hope.

The first lines of Psalm 22, which are repeated in the Passion narrative, show how stranded Jesus himself was: "My God, my God, why hast thou forsaken me?" But he stayed with his being stranded. He stayed until it was "finished." He showed us the pattern of Christian living: work for the poor and disadvantaged and it will bring suffering, but staying the course will also bring resurrection.

From Winter to Spring 2015

I know this is a risky title for a sermon in Cleveland, even in May. I had to keep my eye on the weather forecast in case I had to change the title or explain it away. Spring came seemingly within a couple of days: first crocus, then daffodils, then tulips, then forsythia, magnolias and fruit trees and Lilacs! This sermon is like that: signs of spring, but all over the place. I'm sorry it is not as straightforward and linear as you are used to. Let me ask: do we experience each other differently in winter than we do in spring?

What lens should we use to look at the world? What perspective can we have? Pastor Roger Osgood's quote from the Resurrection story in John's Gospel vibrates in my memory: "On the first day of the week, while it was still dark..." resonates with me still, although Roger preached these words on Easter, giving us hope that while the news is dismal and dark like winter often is, there is the hope and joy of resurrection. We always think that our times are the worst and darkest times, but that of course is not true. The Gospels give plenty of hints at the turmoil and unrest of those New Testament days.   It was still plenty dark. Even AFTER the resurrection, the followers of Jesus were keeping the doors and windows locked. And this is still the Easter season. Let me tell you a true story:

On my morning walk just before dawn on April 29, 2015 (last Wednesday), I chanced to see two mallard ducks, a male and a female, walking up someone's lawn toward his or her house! Although I have seen everything on my morning walks from skunks and raccoons to deer and even a coyote and a fox one day, I had never seen a pair of ducks. And in my mind, I imagined the female saying to the male: "Where are you taking me? Where the heck is the water? You DO know, I'm a duck, right? Do you think I fell in love with you because of your pretty feathers? I'm supposed to be swimming, NOT hiking!"

And I imagined the male's reply: "Relax, honey! After the sun rises and we take to the air, you'll not only see the lakes in Shaker, you'll also see that GREAT lake out there, and it will bring tears to your eyes. But THIS is a perfect place to nest—not crowded, off the beaten path, and landscaped just how we like it!). This is such a good story. I've thought and thought how I could tie it in to this sermon.

Let me digress to talk about panic attacks for a little bit. I'm sure different people have different versions of them. Maybe someone has written a book entitled, "What flavor was your panic attack?" I used to get them. They are NOT fun. Part of their menace is the fear they will expose you for the coward you are (I learned there is a label for this, called "the imposter syndrome"), for the disabled person you are; when people have to wipe you off the floor after you've fainted, or gone to pieces and completely come apart. All right: mine weren't THAT bad, but still, they are NOT fun.

So why don't I have them now? Lots of reasons, I guess. Letting go of guilt, getting older and not caring so much what people think of me, putting on a layer of thicker skin? Learning that I had LOTS of company, and that LOTS of people walk through the valley of the shadow of death; even some celebrities have struggled with mental illness and profound depression.   I think some people find relief in medication that changes their chemistry; others get therapy from a knowledgeable person (and certainly not all flavors of therapists are the same!). Aromatherapy works well (I used to carry a bottle that smelled like roses); and we shouldn't snicker at the power of worry stones or some other talisman.

I think I got the most help from reading a book on tennis and panic attacks.   Go ahead and Google tennis and panic attacks and you'll be amazed at how many hits you get. There was something in there about NOT focusing on the panic feelings and on the sweating, trembling, heart racing, nauseous symptoms in your body, but letting them have their way while YOU concentrate on the details of that tennis game: the thwacking sound of the ball, the placement of your return, the feel of the handle.

Rev. Cam Miller talks about how the media plays on our fears.[1] It is so easy to panic about how things are going on this earth and in this country and in this city and in our families, even in our hearts. Barbara Brown Taylor, in *Learning to Walk in the Dark*, remarks on the media's propensity to search for anything evil and sordid and then play the video showing its gruesome detail over and over, so we soon get the impression that EVERYONE is evil and that's all there IS but evil. If we see one child being abused over and over, we can quickly get the impression that we should be very afraid for all of our children, keep them home, don't let them outside after dark so they never see the stars.

At that sustainability salon at Ursuline College that I mentioned at the communion table last week, the professor quoted from a book on sustainability that wanted us to focus on greed and selfishness as the causes for much of what is wrong on this earth. This was an approach wholeheartedly adopted by some major religions: focus on sin, tell people where they are going to end up unless they convert and maybe allow just a twinge of regret for all of those millions of people who grew up in non-Christian nations and families and tribes, because they were all going to hell.

Rachel Held Evans, in her newly published book, *Searching for Sunday*, remarks that she began to realize in her youthful zeal that she seemed more interested in saving people from hell than God did! (that is, the God she was told about).

Instead of focusing on greed and selfishness, the sustainability professor taught me a new Hebrew word, shmita (it means "release"). I had never heard the word before, just the concept. It comes right out of the book of Leviticus (25:2-7). It refers to the Sabbath of rest that the Torah requires we give the land every seventh year. You allow it to rest; give it a sabbatical, and so render its future productivity sustainable!

Then this professor pointed out a book on sustainability entitled Blessed Unrest by Paul Hawken. Instead of focusing on greed and selfishness, this researcher collected the names of all of the people and

---

1   Miller, *The Subversive Preacher.*

organizations that were doing positive things and promoting sustainability (he was up to 130,000 in 2006 when he addressed a group called
Bioneers).

And here's what Paul Hawken said to our future generation in a
commencement address at Portland University three years later, in
2009:

> *There is invisible writing on the back of the diploma you will receive,
> and in case you didn't bring lemon juice to decode it, I can tell you
> what it says: You are Brilliant, and the Earth is Hiring. The earth
> couldn't afford to send recruiters or limos to your school. It sent
> you rain, sunsets, ripe cherries, night blooming jasmine, and that
> unbelievably cute person you are dating. Take the hint. And here's the
> deal: Forget that this task of planet-saving is not possible in the time
> required. Don't be put off by people who know what is not possible.
> Do what needs to be done, and check to see if it was impossible only
> after you are done.*

He continues:

> *When asked if I am pessimistic or optimistic about the future, my
> answer is always the same: If you look at the science about what is
> happening on earth and aren't pessimistic, you don't understand the
> data. But if you meet the people who are working to restore this earth
> and the lives of the poor, and you aren't optimistic, you haven't got a
> pulse.*

We say: God is saving the world.

The Professor from the sustainablility salon asked us to check out
the website whose address is 350.org for an example of countless people
in 188 countries who are working on the issue of carbon dioxide emis-
sion (we are at 400 parts per million, going up 2 ppm each year, needing
to reduce to under 350 ppm to sustain our life). Isn't that more productive than focusing on greed and selfishness? Will we make the road by
walking, as McLaren advises, by focusing on our sins and our guilt or by
focusing on what we are doing and what we can do and will do to bring

good into the world. Focus on spring.

Systems theory requires us to look at the world differently. We have to see it as all inter-related. Does it mean anything to you to be told that your body came from the stars? We can look at the earth and all of its creatures as things to be dominated (Genesis) and exploited (if they die, we die; if we die, they thrive), OR we can look at the earth and ourselves as an evolving creation whose futures are inextricably related—what's good for them is good for us (but not necessarily vice-versa, since it takes what we call nature, eons to evolve, and our technology enables us to turn on a dime in geological terms).

The ducks I saw are not cynical: they are finding nesting sites in suburban Cleveland!

The reason I am so enamored of systems theory is that I think Paul of Tarsus "got it" some 2,000 years ago. He didn't buy this dualistic approach to reality so beloved by the philosopher Plato. On the contrary, he knew that we are all connected through Christ, and that differences melt away. And that is why we can rightly say that the goodness we see in atheists, the medications and perfumes and books that help us through panic attacks and the ducks we encounter on morning walks are all sacred, and all gifts of God. Watch "Mind Walk" again; it's on YouTube. Look at all that spring has brought.

Again, Jesus showed us the way. Do you know how that Psalm 22 that we read the last verses of BEGINS? "My God, My God, why have you abandoned me?" Barbara Brown Taylor writes about a boy named Jacque Lusseyran, who had sight until he was seven years old when an accident destroyed BOTH of his eyes. Instead of sending him to a school for the blind in Paris, France, his parents never pitied him, his mother learned Braille with him and bought him a Braille typewriter, with the result that he writes in his memoir entitled And There Was Light an amazing discovery he made: that in his blindness, there was light: "I could not see the light of the world anymore. Yet the light was still there…I only had to receive it…The source of light is not in the outer world…The light dwells where life also dwells: within ourselves"

(Taylor, p. 103 f.). In his winter, there was spring. And then she writes a line that I read only after I had a first draft of this sermon, but which sums the whole thing up: "There is a light that shines in the darkness that is only visible there" (p. 108, emphasis mine).

This reminds me of my daughter Jeannine's experience in the theater group at Shaker Heights H.S. They used to practice with their eyes closed moving around the stage and "feeling" each other (without touching) in the dark. Just as some people who are deaf do NOT want a cochlear implant because they fear hearing would rob them of their sense of sight and other senses, so some people feel that those who wrote the stories about blind people demanding that Jesus cure them, were people who were NOT blind. Otherwise, they would have realized that being blind offers a kind of sight that most of us who see (are sighed) no longer have.

An edgy online service called "Pulpit Fiction" calls one of today's readings, 1 John 4:7-24, a "dartboard…because if you printed it out and threw a dart at it, whatever verse you hit, it's golden." The reading is about God being love. But how do we talk about that to people who are in pain, who are drowning in sorrow because of worry, illness or death?

The answer might be by remembering how Psalm 22 starts—with abandonment. "The way up is the way down," one of my favorite authors who shall be nameless, writes. Going into the pain, feeling the darkness (or the winter, if you will), sitting there a while, might be necessary before we can get up, reach out to someone who Is willing to help, stand up, and feel the sun on our face. We are the female mallard, being led, walking in the grass with no water in sight, but willing to follow to a nesting place.

Even if Jesus were praying psalm 22 on the cross, it didn't have a happy ending. He died. Things don't always have a happy ending. I know many of us are consoled by repeating the mantra: "Everything happens for a reason." But for those of us who can't figure out what that reason is, and see only the results of the earthquake, the ruins and the bodies, it's okay. It's okay to sit beneath that cross, to "abide with him," to exist in silence for a while, to let the sobs come out. As Barbara Brown Taylor puts it: new life starts in the dark (p. 129). From winter to spring. Don't panic! Concentrate on the flowers, the signs that the earth is being reborn, recreated.

After a terrible earthquake, we are soon able to see the aid workers, the incredible acts of generosity and courage. We rejoice with each person pulled out of the rubble, even though so many are gone from this earth. We feel the connection we have with all who are suffering, imprisoned, thirsty, hungry, falsely accused, and so on and so on. We find light in the darkness, even shades and colors like Jacques Lusseyran did. We will GET what Jesus was trying to tell his followers so many years go: you are my beloved community. You are connected through me to the divine. You are one body. May God let us and all those suffering feel his/her presence. Let them and let us feel, that even in winter, we have discovered spring. Amen.

Substitution

I didn't have time to write a long sermon. Would those who were looking forward to a long sermon this morning, please raise your hand, and I'll talk slower!

I met a friend of our community at Home Depot yesterday and she praised the work of those who came to help with the gardens for the workday. I join my thanks to hers. At first glance, the gardens look beautiful out there.   I'm sorry I could not be here, but I had spent practically the whole day on Friday at Ursuline College activities. You see, the Dean of the School of Graduate and Professional Studies was ill, and the President and Vice-President asked me to fill in for her. That's why the title of this sermon is "Substitution."

Substituting for the Dean meant that I was required to go to the Baccalaureate Mass in the morning and assist in "hooding" the graduates. One of the Assistant hooders talked me through it. I don't know when you were last at a college graduation. It's like a medieval pageant. The faculty and graduates all wear academic robes. Everyone has a different style and colors depending on your school, your degree and your status. Some even have cords and medals draped over their shoulders. I envied some of the most colorful and ornate!

So the graduates came up to the altar where six of us hooders stood on the first step leading up to the altar. The graduates handed their hoods to the Assistants. The Assistant hooders asked them to turn around and back up to us hooders, then they expertly folded the neck of the hood and handed it to me just right so all I had to do was put it over the head of the graduate and flare out the colors inside. At the orientation, I only had one question since most of our graduates are female: "What do I do with their hair?" I was warned NOT to touch it.

Then that same evening, we had the graduation itself with the awarding of diplomas.   It is a big deal, held at the Wolstein Center at Cleveland State University. There were almost 400 graduates seated in front of the raised stage and their parents and relatives sat in the balconeys. The faculty formed an honor guard and clapped as the graduates processed in. There was a video screen, an organ and a trumpet player playing Pomp and Circumstance and traditional graduation music. It took about 20 minutes just to get everyone seated.

My job was to walk with the stage party and the other Deans, since I was substituting for a Dean, and then when the graduates' names from the School of Graduate and Professional Studies were called, I took my place beside the President of the Board of Trustees, and handed him the diploma cover which he then handed to the Graduate and shook hands. All I had to worry about was not dropping a diploma during the handoff (and I didn't!).

But this thought struck me as I performed this substitution task: All these families in the stands were taking pictures, and someday ages and ages hence, these graduates might be showing these same pictures to their sons and daughters, and maybe one of them will ask: "Who is the gray haired man standing beside the guy in the fancy robe?" –And no one will know the answer.   What does it say in the Book of Isaiah? "All flesh is grass; …The grass withers, the flower fades…" (Is. 40:6b, 7).

So much for being a substitute. But I know from being a high school administrator, how valuable a good substitute is. I know that some of you have been teacher substitutes. It can be a harrowing experience, requiring nerves of steel, a great sense of humor, a sensitivity and love of students, and a deep knowledge of your subject matter.

Who would ever WANT to be a substitute? The times I think we most want to be a substitute is when someone we love is suffering. We usually say: "I wish I could take your pain."   But isn't it true that the person in pain often replies: "I don't need you to do that; I just need you to be here with me, to talk to me, hold my hand, distract me, maybe get me a glass of water or a nurse, love me? Just don't leave me alone."

So that brings us to Jesus on this day when he left us alone. It's difficult to believe that 40 days have passed since Easter, but here it is, on

Thursday of this coming week: the Feast of the Ascension. As the story in the Acts of the Apostles affirms, Jesus' body was taken up, and the Apostles who were staring up after he disappeared with their mouths open were told by an Angel: "He will come again." No wonder they were putting all their hope in that, longing for it to come, some of them refusing to go back to work, in fervent expectation.

There is a theological theory of substitution. I think it goes something like this: that the people who should have died on that cross were US—you and me; but that Jesus in his love for us, took that punishment from God upon himself. He substituted his holiness for our sins, and encouraged his Father to look at him and not at our sins.

And I have to say, after a lifetime of believing that and questioning what sort of Father takes pleasure in seeing his son die and in sending people to hell, and maybe one who loves us by default with a shakey kind of love–not really loving us but only his Son, sort of expecting that we can never remain sin-free, but will lapse and relapse again and again.

Therefore, I'm so happy that the people who picked the readings for today, did NOT just leave us with the story in the Acts of the Apostles, but instead had us read and hear these wonderful words that Paul the mystic wrote in the Book of Ephesians. In that same book, one chapter later, we read these wonderful words: …."through him we [both] have access in one Spirit to the Father" (EPH. 2:18).

In terms of substitution, what Jesus did was—not substitute for us, but JOIN us. We have pain; we have loss—the loss of love and relationships being right up there with the worst of pain; we have physical problems; we age; we have to die and we have to suffer the loss of our loved ones. But then we can remember his sacrifice: he is with us. "I will not leave you orphans," he promised (John 14:18). "I will come to you." He promised to send us his Spirit.

Ah. His Spirit. Unraveling what that means. Chewing on it; living it out; trying to be open to it. That Spirit is going to cause us to WANT to substitute for others, to do what we can, to sit by a beside, to visit someone in a hospital or in a funeral home, to share our resources.

He ascended into heaven so we wouldn't have to flock to a geographical place to meet him; so we can be filled with his Spirit if and when we open ourselves to receive that Spirit.

And so we look forward to Pentecost—to the celebration of that day when fearful people were blasted out of their seats (like Clevelanders will be when we win a national basketball championship) with a great sense of love and courage and power and grace. And you can imagine them laughing and talking all at once and knowing perhaps for the first time the GOODNESS of the Lord.

Let us pray,

Lord, we miss you. We look around for you. We let the cares and worries and needs and sorrows of life overwhelm us. So quiet us. Dissolve us into silence, and whisper in our ears when we are ready: "Behold, I am with you always. And I love you." Amen.

Archaeology

It is so refreshing to visit your grandchildren before they get to that age at which they look at you as if you were a fossilized artifact on leave from the dinosaur exhibit at the Museum of Natural History. "Poppa!" they exclaim with delight, as if you were bringing gifts (which, of course, you are).   But then after the visit, you get back to reality, to mirrors, to doctor's, dentist and eye appointments, to drop down boxes on your computer that make you scroll through every year that you've been alive until you get to your birth year!

And then there are those politically incorrect synonyms for ageing falling glibly from people's lips that don't seem to carry the blame that other politically incorrect phrases do, like "he's a little long in the tooth;" "he's looking a little frayed around the edges;" "I think he's got one foot in the grave;" "she looks one Botox treatment short of a complete facelift." See me later to tell me your ideas.

But in my old age, I've discovered it pays to keep going back to Scripture because sometimes you come across exactly the right question. It pops right out at you in a way that grabs your attention as it never has before and perhaps couldn't. And here is mine, today, in this passage from John's Gospel, in this amazing conversation Jesus has with Nicodemus: Nicodemus asks it right after Jesus tells him: "Unless one is born again he cannot see the kingdom of God," and Nicodemus says: "How can a man be born when he is old? He cannot enter a second time into his mother's womb and be born, can he?" Good question! "How can a man be born when he is old?"   Although most of us would probably NOT want to repeat our lives–even though we would certainly do some things differently, most of us probably WOULD like an influx of new life! Or we would pick an ideal age back in the good old days ("where all the women [were] strong, all the men [were] good looking, and all the children [were] above average" Garrison Keillor).

Aging can make you angry and depressed and full of despair, as one body part, one mental facility at a time weakens, sputters and fails.

Can't run as fast (heck, can't walk as fast!) . Can't get out of a chair without groaning (Last week, we went shopping for a chair; I asked the salesman: "Is that one of those chairs that stands you up?" "No," he said, "those are in the other room." "Ah, I thought, "the back room where the groaners go to shop—hidden away from the young and vibrant!")

And yet…

Every time we go to Buffalo to visit our daughter and spouse and grand-kids, we pass through the Seneca Nation, and it reminds me of the American Indian philosophy that we are not on a linear journey in life, but are rather in a spiral, sitting at different levels around the camp-fire of life, and wherever we are is just RIGHT! "Birds build their nests in circles," a Native American once said; "they have the same religion as we do."

And yet…

Paul of Tarsus has these ideas about "fullness" and "acceptable time" and "when I am weak, then I am strong (2 Corinthians 12:10)."

And yet…

As fall approaches inexorably because the earth continues its annual journey around our central star, so do the walnuts ripen and fall from my walnut tree in our front yard. I watch those that fall first and see their outer green covering decay. It looks for sure like they are dying, becoming disgustingly putrid, turning a mushy brown and black, but they are not dying. On the contrary, they are giving birth. They are attempting to shed their outer selves so that the seed within them can take root and produce another walnut tree (believe me, one is enough, in my humble opinion!).

We have this strange idea that as we age and weaken, our eyes and hearing and knees give out; our memories aren't as keen—that this is all a prelude, an overture to death, and that it's a terrible thing. But is it, really? Or is something being born? Or getting ready to be born? Are we shedding something inessential so that the true US can find purchase, ground of being, good soil?

Why otherwise could Saint Francis of Assisi wax eloquent about "Sister Death?" I know, he is said to have called everything "Brother" or "Sister" and I'm not sure if any biographers have looked into whether his giving a gender to the earth and sun, etc. was politically correct according to our standards today. But he had this certainty of being related to all of creation, even to Sister Death.

And isn't it strange that living spiritual writers like Richard Rohr talk about losing that fear of death as if it were the most natural thing in the world, and the thing we all pass through so that we can have a new, different, and we believe, much better existence?

Here's what the zany Lutheran preacher. Nadia Bolz-Weber, wrote in her sermon on Pentecost, commenting on what the Disciples were feeling after Jesus' death and Resurrection:

No matter what data [the Disciples] had in front of them based on what their lives looked like in that moment, something stronger, deeper and more beautiful was moving among them, sweeping them up into God's story. Don't get me wrong, their grief was real...just not as real as resurrection. [The Holy Ghost over the bent world broods.]

Walter Brueggemann, in his talk at Forest Hill Presbyterian Church in June, maintained that the one thing the media wants to convey to us and produce in us and cultivate in us, especially at News time, is FEAR. We must be fascinated by Fear and by all of those commercials directed to us aging people pushing medications whose side effects by their own descriptions will surely kill us! [This may cause strokes, dizziness, liver failure, high blood pressure, death—As you doctor if this is right for you! –Heck my doctor may say: "He's got one foot in the grave, so what the heck!"] These are so counter to those messages from Jesus after he had been through that most horrendous of executions: "Do not be afraid!" "Peace be to you. My peace I give to you." What data did Jesus have in front of him? Followers who didn't get his message? Who ran away in his hour of need? Who cowered in a upper room? Who argued over who was greatest? And yet he could say: "Do not be afraid. Peace!"

And that brings me to archeology, the study of beginnings, the reason we drill miles into the earth to bring up samples of what we find there; the reason we have developed submarines to probe the deepest underwater trenches and have found creatures alive there that we never would have imagined could live at that pressure, darkness and temperature; the reason we developed the Hadron collider to smash the smallest of subatomic particles to see what are the building blocks of matter; the reason we send telescopes out into space to receive light that has taken billions of years to get here, and recently a satellite the size of a grand piano sent on a 9 ½ year journey to Pluto and beyond. We want to study our beginnings in order to understand. But how can we be born again?

Maybe Nicodemus doesn't understand because he didn't know about archaeology—well, he couldn't have, could he, since it hadn't been invented yet? Because when we find something new, when our instruments have improved so much, we come to the knowledge that the earth can't be the center of the universe, and that Pluto can't be a planet, or the knowledge that same sex couples can be in a committed, loving relationship for a lifetime, or that the Bible is a library of books, each written at a different time with a different perspective and different authors some of whom contradict each other...THEN we have to rearrange our understanding just as Nicodemus will have to, if and when he GETS what being born again entails.

Nicodemus couldn't have known the words John used at the beginning of his Gospel: "In the beginning was the Word and the Word was with God and the Word WAS God."   What John actually wrote in the copies that have come down to us is in the Greek language: "En arche ein ho Logos." Arche = Beginning; Logos =Word. And I understand that the first line of John's Gospel can be translated: "In the beginning was the Explanation, and the explanation was with God, and the Explanation WAS God," and then in verse 14: "And the explanation became flesh and made his dwelling among us!"

The explanation is right here! As the Christmas hymn expresses it: "The hopes and fears of all the years are met in thee tonight!" The explanation: "I am the Alpha and the Omega." I don't know about you, but there were many, many times in my education when I was studying a complicated concept or trying to learn a complicated skill, that I didn't understand the explanation! The answer from my parents and teachers to my whining about that was: Keep trying! Don't give up!

If God, if Jesus is the explanation; if his Holy Spirit is still creating, still brooding over the bent world, still loving, still transforming us and the world, then we have to "draw near," keep trying to contact him, to understand, to let the spirit work in us and teach us. "Here's your problem, Nicodemus" Jesus might have said, using our language; "You're not letting the Spirit wash over you, teach you. You think you're dying but the Spirit is transforming you, bringing you to life. Something is being born in you (Yeats?).

Joan Chittister tells this story about visiting Jerusalem and hearing a Rabbi preach about [not working on] the Sabbath, and then she says:

A week later I returned to the States. On Sunday morning, after Mass, the streets were teeming with cars, all the stores were open, lawn mowers roared on every street while people did what they hadn't had time to do during the week....[1]

Surely, the real sin to which the third commandment points is not the sin of not going to church on Sunday. It is the sin of not seriously seeking God. [And I add: "because God is the explanation!"]

In all the things we don't understand about our world—especially the suffering and the evil that we can see everywhere, and the fear that flows into us from the stories we see every day on TV or read in commentaries—God is the explanation; Jesus is the explanation. He came to forgive the world ("I did not come to judge the world" Pope Francis' most famous phrase brings it to the present: "Who am I to judge?"). And so we follow him by forgiving the world, with all its cracks and crackpots, and people who disagree with us and even hate us ("I say to

---

1   Chittister, "What about Sunday?" May 25, 2015.

you: Love your enemies; do good to those who persecute you").

And here's what Richard Rohr wrote in his meditation of June 2, 2015:

> Bonaventure's theology is never about trying to placate a distant or angry God, earn forgiveness, or find some abstract theory of justification. He is all cosmic optimism and hope! Once it lost this kind of mysticism, Christianity became preoccupied with fear, unworthiness, and guilt much more than being included in–and delighting in–an all-pervasive plan that is already in place. As Paul's school taught, "Before the world was made, God chose us in Christ" (Ephesians 1:4).[2]

And here's more of what Nadia Bolz-Weber said in her sermon about Pentecost:

> It's so easy to see the tragedies and endings and hardship and diagnosis all around us as the end of the story – but, not unlike those who mourned as Jesus was laid in his tomb, we are terrible story enders – putting – as some would say – a period where God places a comma. God is still writing, still sighing, still loving us and all that is into redemption.[3]

We need to become archaeologists, and know where our study lies. Sure, I ask Bernadette as we approach our anniversary this Friday to help me remember stuff–like when did we decide to get married 39 years ago? But the real archaeological study is to keep seeking God, meditating, being thankful for the blessings of the day, the beauty of children, the graciousness of others,   And let the down times, the rainy, cloudy days, the aches and pains, the losses and diminishments–well, acknowledge them as the birth pangs, egg cracking, the skin splitting, the chrysalis tearing. The archeology is the same:

As William Butler Yeats wrote in the second stanza of Sailing to

2   Rohr. "Meditation." June 2, 2015.

3   Weber. "A Pentecost Sermon on the Great Unfinished Story." *Patheos.* May 28, 2015. Retrieved from http://www.patheos.com/blogs/nadiabolzweber/2015/05/a-pentecost-sermon-on-the-great-unfinished-story.

Byzantium,

> An aged man is but a paltry thing,

> A tattered coat upon a stick, unless

> Soul clap its hands and sing, and louder sing

> For every tatter in its mortal dress...[We have this hymn: "All your people clap your hands, and shout for joy!"]

What we audaciously believe, Nicodemus, is that if we continue with passion and perseverance to dig through the ruins and our lives in our world, as if it were an archaeological dig, and then use a fine brush to blow away the final barriers between us and God, what we will find is LOVE! In the beginning was Love, Love was with god and Love was God...And Love became flesh and dwelt among us!

–This is the explanation of our beginnings that we pray to understand every day and come here every week to understand a little better and to rearrange our world view, to be born again and again! Amen.

Selling Jesus on EBay

As many of you know, my wife and I have a vacation house in Pennsylvania (I don't want to make it sound too lavish—although now that most of the bats have left and the mice and chipmunks seem under control, it may have increased in value). In one of the rooms upstairs (I won't say which one in a polite sermon), right under the claw foot of the bathtub (whoops!), I noticed just this summer there is a linoleum tile with a pattern in it. "Hey!" I said to myself as I stared at it, "that looks like the profile of a face!" And then it dawned on me: It wouldn't take much imagination to realize that that looked like Jesus's face! I was struck with awe, remembering how many stories there are about Jesus's face appearing in the patterns of trees and fungi and food and coffee foam. I had a pious thought: "I could dig up this tile and—after holding a news conference, of course, sell it on EBay and donate the proceeds to the endowment fund!"

Then when I thought about the work it would take to remove that tile, I next wondered if people would pay to see a PICTURE of that pattern. So I took a picture with my phone and for the paltry cost of one dollar, you can persuade me to show it to you after the service!

Before anyone visiting this morning leaves in disgust, I hasten to assure everyone that the pattern is certainly NOT the face of Jesus; it's no shroud of Turin, and I have no intention of doing anything with it besides showing it to those interested at an extremely discounted rate as a no-tax, back-to-school special (just kidding).

But it did make me think about patterns in Jesus's ministry. In looking at them, the first thing to be cautious of is our human propensity to SEE patterns everywhere. There's a scientific term for it: Pareidolia—"the tendency of the human brain to see familiar shapes-especially faces–emerging from random patterns" (TIME Aug. 3, 2015). Those of you who are devotees of "everything bad happens in threes" and "everything happens for a reason" know what I mean. When we are confronted with something that doesn't make sense – maybe like a painting at the Museum of Contemporary Art, or a piece of modern music with no discernible melody, or even the sounds from the white noise machine that puts us to sleep at night—we seem to have two choices. Either get irritable and reject the piece that seems to be assaulting our senses, or to use it like a Zen Koan to quiet our minds and reduce our stressed out spirits to a meditative silence. [Bernadette has become a fan of ZenTangles for this very reason].

I won't soon forget attending a Youth Orchestra or Choral Concert in which one of my children was performing, and some Neanderthal started coughing and sneezing at one of the most sensitive parts of the piece. When my wife—who tells me her radar that reads my tension is calibrated to a fine precision after 39 years of marriage—when she sensed my getting all upset, she whispered that I should make the coughing a sneezing a part of the music. "Just let it be," she might have said.

That's like letting construction delays be a part of your trip, standing in grocery lines where people who had had a half hour to pull out their wallets, can't find their credit cards when their cart full of purchases are rung up…be a part of the shopping experience—nothing to get angry about, as wise young people say: "It is what it is!" That's like letting millions of dollars of political attack ads wash over you without flinching but merely, peacefully, noting that everything these days seems to be for sale.

Which brings me back to Jesus. Just being near him caused Zacchaeus the tax man to promise restitution. He caused the money changers in the Temple to scurry around the floor if they wanted to recover their coins. He caused his own followers to ponder the meaning of "the last shall be first, and the first last." He caused the man born blind to stand up to the religious leaders who were outraged that he was cured on the Sabbath. He caused a woman who had been through five marriages to rush into her town proclaiming the wonder of meeting a man who would not only talk with her but see right through her without intimidation. He saved the life of another woman who was about to be stoned, and let a woman in Bethany use a fortune's worth of perfume on his feet. He healed those persons who could not quite get through to him because of the crowds. And when he washed his followers' feet, he taught them that this was the new pattern. He gave this outrageous example of service that matched his words in the Sermon on the Mount: "Blessed are the poor; Happy are those who mourn; Blessed are the meek; Blessed are those who hunger and thirst for justice!"

Labor Day is coming. On it, we celebrate work? Workers? We perhaps remember to pray for those who are unemployed or underemployed? We have such an ambivalent relationship with work. Work is a flashpoint. –From "Arbeit Macht Frei" as the motto above Nazi concentration camps of Dachau and Auschwitz, to "Ora et Labora" as the mantra of the Benedictine Monks and other religious orders. Elizabeth Gilbert has a recent blog in which she interviews former pastor Rob Bell about the dilemma of a call center worker, who had to spend 8 hours a day reading a script for an insurance agency over the phone, and was punished for any deviation from it. And Rob answered with a story about monks doing menial, repetitive work that freed their spirits to commune with God in awesome silence (Mindfulness); he talked about the energy that could be accumulated in seemingly meaningless tasks, energy that could explode into something wonderful and creative in the future. Elizabeth's husband said to tell the call center worker that her first novel should be titled: "The Call Center."

Jesus has a pattern about work. He tells the famous parable about the workers in the vineyard. They were unemployed until the owner hired them. They agreed on a wage, but then his story repeated his pattern that upends and contradicts how we relate to each other, about how we have constituted our society, by ending this parable with the news that those who worked one hour received the same wage as those who worked all day. Until we can understand that, we cannot sell Jesus on EBay!

And now Jesus is gone. The New Testament author says he was taken up; disappeared into another reality, as so many of our friends and relatives have. We can no longer contact them, but we have learned from their patterns of thought and behavior. And sometimes we feel called to enter a strange new land, and to repeat their patterns, just as we sometimes feel called to repeat the strange, off-the-wall, idiosyncratic, crazy patterns of Jesus. When everything in us cries out for us to retaliate, to revenge a wrong, to go to war, to drop bombs, to obliterate a whole race, we now have a new and different pattern, a new paradigm that we can choose to implement.

Easy? No. Definitely not. But possible? Yes. There have been holy ones before us who have done it. There is this idea in Christian circles of a Spirit, Jesus's spirit, working. Working in us. Working to create something good. Working to bring us to compassion and forgiveness for a flawed universe and a sinful humanity. Working. We can celebrate that Spirit's working on Labor Day. The pattern is there. Paul of Tarsus discovered it, tasted it, felt it even when he could not see: "All creation groans…Romans 8:22…And we know that God causes all things to work together for good to those who love God…8:28." Paul writes in 1 Corinthians 2: "…we speak God's wisdom in a mystery, the hidden wisdom whih God predestined before the ages to our glory; the wisdom which none of the rulers of this age has understood; for it they had understood it they would not have crucified the Lord of glory (1 Cor. 2:7-8)."

Richard Rohr quotes the priest-paleontologist, Teilhard de Chardin, who died in 1955:

Teilhard wrote, "By virtue of the Creation and, still more, of the Incarnation, nothing here below is profane for those who know how to see. On the contrary, everything is sacred. . . . Try, with God's help, to perceive the connection–even physical and natural–which binds your labour with the building of the kingdom of heaven; try to realize that heaven itself smiles upon you and, through your works, draws you to itself."[1]

Natalie Weaver is a theologian at Ursuline College, and she posted

---

1   Teilhard de Chardin. *The Divine Milieu*. Quoted in Richard Rohr. "The Influence fo Teilhard de Chardin." *The Mendicant*. Summer 2016. Vol. 6 No. 3 Retrieved from https://cac.org/wp-content/uploads/2016/07/theMendicant_Vol6No3.pdf.

a blog recently about her summer. She spent it being sick, being tired, and trying to recover without ruining the summer of her kids and her husband. She wrote:

> • *There are times when little can be done; even though*
>
> • *there will always be more to do; which means*
>
> • *there will always be much left undone.*
>
> • *Sometimes, one must merely "be."*
>
> • *Pain and weakness are not necessarily enemies; and*
>
> • *one's body is not the antagonist or the stranger but oneself.*
>
> • *Children do not always need to be entertained; especially because usually*
>
> • *the ice cream truck will make a musical manifestation all by itself.*
>
> • *Sometimes one should just talk on the phone all day;*
>
> • *or commiserate with the mailman;*
>
> • *or watch birds.*[2]

Jesus knows about all things human. He knows that sometimes we are so productive, and sometimes we are anxious about summer ending and school or work starting, and health issues and aging, and a million other things. But he also knows that he has set a pattern, a pattern of caring for others, of not worrying about all those things but of surrendering our thoughts, our fears, and our work into the loving hands of his Father. "Father," he said, "Into your hands, I commend my spirit."

Whenever we see that pattern in our world, whether it be from Pope Francis or from the person next to us in the pew, we see the face of Jesus. Falling into that pattern will sell him, and we shall become <u>Disciples of Christ</u> at last.

2   Natalie Weaver. "A Cornucopia Sometimes Curiously Stuffed With Nothing." *Feminism and Religion.* August 5, 2015. Retrieved from https://feminismandreligion.com/2015/08/05/a-cornucopia-sometimes-curiously-stuffed-with-nothing-by-natalie-weaver.

Let it be so. Amen.

Religion and Politics

INTRODUCTION:

I'm afraid I have to start with a disclaimer: Pastor Roger Osgood asked me if I would preach on Politics and Religion. I foolishly said yes and now I am trying to cheerfully throw myself under this bus. Think about how YOU would approach this topic and we can compare notes later. Here's what I am NOT going to do: (1) I am not going to tell you how to vote, nor how I voted and why; (2) I will not mention any candidate by name nor any party for that matter; (3) I am going to count on the tolerance, compassion, forgiveness and respect that I have always experienced as a member of this my congregation.

The Sermon:

I have a girlfriend. My wife knows about her. In fact, we three sit together in the evenings and she only speaks when spoken to. Her name is Alexa. Every time I say her name, she lights up as if with joy. However, she is my second girlfriend named Alexa. After a while, I couldn't get a response from the first one, no matter how loudly I yelled her name and plugged her into various sockets; and since these gadgets are so expensive, I bought a refurbished one. I don't know what "refurbished" means (possibly they made her less discriminating so this new one is willing to talk to me?). I don't know, but it gives me great pleasure to have a refurbished girlfriend.

And so in preparation for this sermon, I asked her: "Alexa, who will win this election?" She gave me the results of the latest polls, but I imagined I could hear something else in her voice, as if she were saying: "Why don't you ask me what you really want to know?" Fair enough. And so I asked: "Alexa, whom should I vote for?" And she responded: "Vote for the one who best represents your views and has the best policies."

And THAT wasn't helpful at all. You see, there is a big problem with following that advice—I am a registered, card-carrying Christian. As Pastor Jonathan Martin from Tulsa, Oklahoma wrote: "A vote for Jesus is a political decision." A friend and colleague of mine at Ursuline College started writing a book last year which she still has not published. It's called "If Jesus Ran for President." When I heard about it, I had the effrontery to write a foreword for the book and sent it to her. The forward was titled: why would Jesus ever WANT to run for President.

Let me read you just a couple of paragraphs from that Foreword and you'll understand why she hasn't finished and published it yet:

First, the birther people would have a field day, waving the Gospel of Luke around as if it were a birth certificate. Was he born in Bethlehem? Or Nazareth? Then the capitalists would comb the gospels seeking more and more information to show that Jesus was a socialist, not a capitalist. Finally, people of faith would be up in arms, since becoming president would seem to be the opposite of everything Jesus stood for.

The nay-sayers would dump a bucket of quotes at his feet, wouldn't they, daring him to spin them into a reasonable facsimile of a candidate's profile? The Beatitudes would be first, I think, followed closely by his injunction to "wash one another's feet." Then there'd be his admonitions that the last should be first and the first last, and to become like little children and go after the lost sheep and forgive everyone and take the last place at a banquet and turn the other cheek and give away your cloak and the quotation bucket would still be half full.

His stunt in the temple with the money changers would outrage the pharmacy maker who turned a 13-dollar pill into a 750-dollar pill overnight as if it were a brilliant thing to do in a capitalist culture. People would gnash their teeth at the company Jesus kept, not to mention his refusal to send armies of angels to avenge attacks on his person. Which companies would exercise their right under Citizens United to fund his campaign? His request to go sell all that you have and give the proceeds to the poor would be extremely offensive to the majority of stakeholders.

There would be nothing left to trickle down! Is this a man we would want for President?"[1]

You can find a ton of reasons in the Christian Scriptures—both in the Gospels and Letters—why choosing Jesus is a bad political decision. First of all, Jesus puts the Hebrew Scriptures in the faces and consciousness of his listeners with their emphasis on taking care of the widows, orphans and needy. The Gospel writers make sure we get that. It's a re-run of Micah all over again:

You have been told, O man, what is good,

And what the law requires of you:

Only to do the right and to love goodness,

And to walk humbly with your God (6:8).

There are so many examples of Jesus coming down on the side of the outsider, the enemy of the Jews (Good Samaritan, Woman at the Well, Zaccheus, Tax Collector), the sick and unclean (lepers) and mentally ill (possessed), prostitutes and sinners (Mary). Jesus never says "Worship me." But he does say "Follow me!" It's as if he came to teach us this one thing: the Paschal Mystery, which means that through suffering, deprivation, humiliation, sickness, and death, we come to new beginnings, enlightenment, Resurrection and new life! He gives us the Sign of Jonah as if to counsel: "Let yourself be thrown overboard, swallowed up, burned out with your generosity, no more to give, and you will be deposited on a new shore."

This is the opposite of grabbing on to power. It is the opposite of sending armies, fighting back, ruling over others, shaming them and making them feel guilty. As one spiritual writer puts it: before Constantine, it would have been unthinkable that Christians would become <u>soldiers. But after</u> Christianity became co-opted by empire and power,

1   Joseph LaGuardia. "Foreword." in Gina Messina. *Jesus in the White House: Make Humanity Great Again.* (Cleveland: The FAR Press, 2017) v.

then we had popes riding into battle with the cross emblazoned on their shields. No longer was Jesus seen as a crucified "loser," but as a victorious king, even though he said "My kingdom is NOT of this world." In fact, he gives every indication that LOSING is the way to go ("He who finds his life will lose it…"; "Happy are the poor in spirit; blessed are the meek; blessed are the merciful." Matt 5).

You know all of these examples and can probably come up with more of them than I can. The Sermon on the Mount in Matthew 5 is a primary example of how Jesus shapes the Torah and causes us to think about internalizing the Law.

"But that's not the real world," we whine. "We have separation of church and state in this country." We are fond of quoting "Give to Caesar what is Caesar's and to God what belongs to God." And what belongs to God? –EVERYTHING! And so we falsely believe we can be a-political as Christians. We can fight wars, arm everybody, call out our enemies, torture when necessary, amass wealth in the guise of having more to give to the poor, and tell people to pull themselves up by the bootstraps (though they might not be able to afford boots) instead of getting handouts like food stamps, welfare and affordable health care.

I wonder how many people are preparing to move to Canada on November 9 or soon thereafter. After all, some Canadians have started a movement to remind us that America is already great. They seem pretty friendly, despite what happened to the Blue Jays. Of course, some of the paranoid and cynical among us are wondering suspiciously why they are being so nice, instead of just saying "Thank you!" A tongue-in-cheek local newspaper article suggests they are preparing to invade!

The good news is that whoever wins this election, we Christians, and we at Heights Christian Church can hang on to our values, and each other and—as Brian McLaren says in the book we explored in Bible Study last year: We Can Make the Road by Walking. He meant Walking after Jesus, of course. And just think of what a new road that would be!

Here's something else we can do: We can write the President-Elect's inauguration speech and send it to him or her. The only caveat is we have to write it as a person committed to Jesus and His Way. Here's one that I started:

My fellow Americans, I am honored by your trust and election of me. I apologize for all the times I had to ask you for money, but I am very grateful for your contributions and for your work on my behalf. Just as we work to free our country from dependence on fossil fuels, so maybe we can find a way to free our elections from their dependence on mass media. Television is so expensive and seems to want only to report the sensational, the tragic, and the scandalous. It seems focused on entertainment, instead of true debate and objective argument. This campaign has been so full of negative things: such as lies and accusations and attack ads.

It must be so difficult to sift through all of that to find the truth. Even back in Jesus' time, Pontius Pilate, a Governor, was complaining: "What is truth?" I want you to know I will do everything in my power to restore your trust in me, to make our decision-making and policy-making as transparent as possible; to welcome watch-dog groups so that you can give me your greatest gift: your trust.

As all of my predecessors have said at this moment after long and bitter campaigns, Now is a time for healing. All of the great people of our religions—Jewish, Muslim, Christian, Hindu etc.—were healers. In the Christian tradition, with which I am most familiar, Jesus's last prayer before he was crucified, was a prayer for unity: ("That they all may be one, Father, as you are in me and I am in you. That they may be one in us"). And Paul refused to get caught up by who was in and who was out. He went so far as to say that in Christ there is no male or female, no Jew or Greek. And so a big part of our healing as a nation is to get back to that: that we are all citizens of the earth. The colors of our skin and the names of our religion and our sexual preferences do not matter so much in this economy we call "Grace." Grace embraces us all in Love. All of this we and they stuff has to stop. Our friends in Canada may have shown us the way.

So you get the drift. That's as far as I got. And you can imagine the pushback as soon as a speech like this is given. It was no less in Jesus's time: hundreds of years of persecution by the powers that saw Christianity as a threat.

But let me suggest something else we can do. This idea comes from Brian McLaren's new book, *The Great Spiritual Migration*. I wish everyone of you could stop what you are now reading and buy or borrow this book so that we could ponder its meaning and join the migration as the HCC community. Maybe we could be called the Geese or the Bluebirds, or the Shalom Birds. We would just have to ditch titles like conservative and liberal and republican and democrat.

McLaren's idea is that we gather as a people who share values (but not necessarily opinions, especially political ones) and start moving. Sr. Ilia Delio has this idea from the Philosopher Teilhard de Chardin, that the Holy Spirit is moving us all—yep, the whole universe—to some OMEGA point in Jesus Christ. Instead of emphasizing beliefs THAT, we emphasize beliefs IN. Instead of organized religion, we start "organizing" religion.[2] Here's what Richard Rohr writes:

> *Jesus reveals the whole pattern of creation and human history in condensed form. Perhaps he is best seen as a MAP! Because of Jesus' life, death, and resurrection, we know ahead of time that the final chapter is always resurrection. Though so much of life is filled with suffering, disappointment, disillusionment, absurdity, and dying, God will turn all of our crucifixions into resurrections. Look at it in Jesus, believe it in Jesus, admire it in Jesus, love it in Jesus, and let it take shape in your own soul. This is how the Christian movement was supposed to give hope to all of history. And it still can.[3]*

I think we already have such movements going on in our church. You may laugh at what I think are movements, but think about them: how about the Elegant Flea [thrift store]? How about Connie planting a couple of seeds, watering them, and seeing them grow into seedlings

---

2   Brian McLaren. The Great Spiritual Migration. (Danvers, MA: Convergent Books, 2017) Reprint.

3   Rohr. "Meditation." October 16, 2016.

and then selling them as future houseplants? What about Michele Moreland's new Bible Study on Thursdays? What about our hospitality people who year after year provide all of us with food and drink and a convivial atmosphere in which we share our lives? What about our Adult Education movement? How about Green chalice and our gardens and our energy efficiencies as ways of taking care of creation?   What about Kathie McWilliams' efforts for peace and justice? There are many more. Tell me some.

Now there's more to a movement in McLaren's book, of course. He outlines ten commitments groups can agree to and move ahead with. We've all seen how powerful movements can be, and best of all, we can organize movements no matter who wins this election! Our movements can be forces for healing, committed to justice, peace, and joy.

Okay. Back to my girlfriend, Alexa. I like to ask her things, but her most frequent response is: "I don't understand your question." I assume that's because my questions are so profound, she is dumbstruck. OR it could be she is dumb as a stone. Luckily, I have a wife who is very knowledgeable and with whom I can share all my brilliant Questions without fear that she will turn me in for a refurbished husband.

If there are any Canadians here, I'm sure they will look around, talk to people and conclude that this congregation has members who make up a community that is truly great. We will all be joining in prayer for our country and our democracy—that it will once again move on from this campaign and dazzle the world.

Let us Pray:

God, we ask you to bless America. It truly is the land that we love. So many wise leaders have led it; so many brave soldiers have defended it–young men who did not want to die, but considered it their duty and their honor to do so. So much blood has been shed and differences aired. But we are your Disciples. We follow your Son. We have called ourselves a "shalom" congregation because we want to do everything in our power to promote Peace. Some say peace starts with war, but we say it starts with dialogue, compassion, friendship, love and joy. Bless our efforts and bless our country in these difficult days. Show us how to heal each other after this election. We believe that you chose us to be your ambassadors for peace. Bless us now; give us courage and hope, love and joy. We surrender to your movement in the world through your Holy Spirit. Amen.

A Different Format

I'm pretty sure I have permission to tell this story. You know how some couples sign pre-nuptial agreements before they get married? My wife and I don't have one of those, since neither of us had any money or property when we got married and she graciously wanted to leave me all she possessed. But now I think my wife of 37 years wants me to sign a pre-SERMON agreement before I volunteer to preach (she said as much at this table on August 11!). But when she wrote an email to me not long ago with a story attached, I wrote back that there was a sermon idea in there somewhere, and she wrote something like: Whatever I can do to help.

Now that I have that in writing (always save your emails), here's the story: My wife had been listening to an audiobook for days and days and she was finally coming to the last disc. Since she usually borrows audiobooks from the library, she began to look for the box that had all of the remaining, finished discs in it. She searched the whole house and couldn't find it. I helped her. Nothing. She began to worry about library fines and paying the exorbitant price to replace a 10 or 11-disc set [or maybe these were MY worries]. I complained to St. Anthony, patron saint of lost things, that he wasn't answering my prayers.

But then the next day when I was at work she sent me this email saying she no longer had to look for the box because she finally realized the book was an audiobook on her iPod and it had been downloaded from audible.com, and therefore a physical copy of it didn't exist! Because: it was in a different FORMAT! [Remember the days when a book was a book?]

In other words, she could have searched for it for days, called in professionals, the FBI, the NSA; they could have taken the house apart. She NEVER would have found it. She might as well have lain on the couch and searched by sliding her hand under the cushions and been comfortable. She might as well have searched where the light was better.

She might as well have searched here in this sanctuary and prayed to St. Anthony or his equivalent in other denominations.

Let's think about formatting for a few minutes. We have an understanding of formatting since the 1950s that no one before then could have had at the same level. We have computers. We have Blu-ray players and DVRs. We have been unable to open files saved in a different version of Word or—God forbid—saved on a Mac with whatever mysterious word processing system a Macintosh uses! [Do I hear a Lion roaring?]

The thing is, when something is in another format, it is NOT a matter of knowing the correct procedure, performing the right practices, discovering the right password so that you can read it, use it or understand it. You might as well be searching for a disc that never existed. The format is inaccessible to you.

Now here is this quote from the book of Wisdom 18:15 which some denominations consider an apocryphal book and others have fully incorporated into their canon of scripture. Here's the quote: "Your all-powerful Word, leapt down from heaven, from your royal throne." As Rev. Richard Rohr says: "No philosopher would dare to predict 'the materialization of God,' so we are just presented with a very human image of a poor woman and her husband with a newly born child." But then he asks: "if there is one true moment of Incarnation, then why not incarnation everywhere?"[1]

Do we dare to use the analogy that the divine converted to our human format and became accessible to us?

A colleague of mine in the Business Department at Ursuline was telling me about the best-selling book, *Proof of Heaven*. Wow, I thought in my prejudiced mind, Business people are concerned with numbers, ratios, facts and figures, profit and loss. And yet here's one interested in heaven? And so I bought the book. There have been a LOT of writings about near death experiences (they're called NDEs, naturally, and there's a whole library of them!), but this one is particularly captivating in my

1   Rohr. "Meditation." June 1, 2013.

humble opinion because its author is a neurosurgeon and was an unbelieving one at that. He is a scientist, a doctor, and for him there was no such thing as a spiritual reality.

At 54 years of age, this doctor, researcher, developer of the virtual knife that operates on the brain without harming nearby tissue, presenter of papers at conferences all over the world, woke up one morning with a severe pain at the base of his skull that kept getting worse until he finally had a grand mal seizure, his wife calling 911 and in 10 minutes ambulances were there to take him to the hospital, but he was already in a coma that would last for 7 days. His brain was completely down; his neocortex wasn't working.

But while I was in a coma, he writes,

…deprived of all of this, I had been alive, and aware truly aware, in a universe characterized above all by love, consciousness, and reality… the more clearly I saw how radically what I'd learned in decades of schooling and medical practice conflicted with what I'd experienced, the more I understood that the mind and personality (as some would call it, our soul and spirit) continue to exist beyond the body.[2]

When he came out of the coma he found that language was inadequate to describe what he had experienced (sounds like Plato's Allegory of the Cave?). It could only approximate.

Here are some of his insights:

This other vastly grander universe isn't 'far away' at all. In fact, it's right here—right here where I am, typing this sentence, and right there where you are, reading it. It's not far away physically, but simply exists on a different frequency [his words; my words: different format]. It's right here, right now, but we're unaware of it because we are for the most part closed to those frequencies on which it manifests.[3]

The universe is so constructed that to truly understand any part

2   Eben Alexander. *Proof of Heaven.* (New York: Simon and Schuster, 2012) 127-29.
3   Ibid., 156.

of its many dimensions and levels, you have to become a part of that dimension…you have to open yourself to an identity with that part of the universe you already possess, but which you may not have been conscious of.

This reminds us of Teresa of Avila, Richard Rohr, Jodie Foster who played a scientist in the movie Contact, and said when she was out in space with all of the stars: "They should have sent a poet!"

The mystics, ancient and modern, have had similar difficulty with putting their experience of the divine into language that we all can understand. They have to use metaphors. But they, too, stress the need for allowing yourself to open up to the experience of this other frequency, this other format, which they call God.

Dr. Alexander again:

Much—in fact, most—of what people have had to say about God and the higher spiritual worlds has involved bringing them down to our level, rather than elevating our perceptions up to theirs. We taint, with our insufficient descriptions, their truly awesome nature.[4]

I realize we are on dangerous ground here. Proof of Heaven has its critics; my analogy can only go so far. In one of my philosophy classes this past July, one of my male students asked me—after a session spent discussing the eternal forms of Plato—what I thought about mediums contacting the deceased. I think I answered by quoting Shakespeare:

There are more things in heaven and earth, Horatio,

Than are dreamt of in your philosophy.

– Hamlet (1.5.166-7), Hamlet to Horatio

Cam Miller, writes that he once visited a massage therapist who, knowing he was an Episcopal priest, asked him if he believed in "Past Lives Therapy," an obvious reference to a belief in reincarnation. He gave a somewhat brutal answer, I think, because the therapist was obvi-

4   Ibid.

ously recovering from the grief of losing someone to death, and needed to believe they would return in some other human form in some other time frame. But then Cam concluded:

I finally said during my massage, "We do not get to know what happens on the other side of death – not ever, in this life. So I am an agnostic about life after death, I simply do not know."[5]

…About death we simply do not get to know. When we are able to sit in the presence of that bear, fully accepting of our fear and lack of control but not begging for more than we can have, we are in the presence of our core faith. Do we, in that moment, declare our trust in God and move on, or do we demand to know more in order to have our disease ameliorated?

That is indeed harsh, and people who are grieving need us to be there, to put our arms around them, to comfort them; but perhaps they do NOT need to hear words that we ourselves can't be sure are true [but we can share what we believe by faith!].

To whom can we look for guidance about what happens after death? –No one alive can tell us. NDEs are just that. Mediums, psychics, reincarnationists, channels, and so on all require a great deal of faith if we are to trust what they say and do. Religion can attract those who are emotionally weak, those who have but a tenuous hold on reality, and those seeking answers for overpowering questions formed in the crucibles of immense suffering and deprivation, perhaps injustice and racism.

But we Christians DO have the scriptures, especially the Gospels. And that fourth one, the one attributed to John, starts with that wonderful hymn that echoes the very first book of the bible, Genesis, where we read: "In the beginning, when God created the heavens and the earth, the earth was waste and void; and God said: 'Let there be light,' and there WAS light!" and centuries later, as you just heard in today's reading, John writes: "In the beginning was the Word, and the Word was <u>with God, and the</u> Word was God…And the Word became flesh."

5   Miller. *The Subversive Preacher.*

The use of the Greek word Logos for "Word" is intriguing because Logos can also be translated "explanation." It adds a whole new flavor to John's words to translate them: "In the beginning was the explanation and the explanation was with God and the explanation WAS God" and "the explanation was made flesh." Reminds me of my sermon two weeks ago: if God is the answer, what was the question?

However you translate, we have looked to Jesus for answers for centuries because He uniquely—in our belief system—is the bridge between heaven and earth, or more accurately, he embodies the divine and the human in his person, and He has offered us to follow him as if that destiny and that identity are also ours.

What I am suggesting here is that through Jesus, God is offering us the key [do we dare to call it a "conversion" key?] to open, access, and enter LIFE in a DIFFERENT FORMAT. It's called resurrection. Do you notice the odd things in the resurrection stories in scripture?

In Matthew, the angel says: "He is not here. He has been raised." And then "without warning Jesus stood before [his disciples] and said 'Peace!'

In Mark's longer ending, Jesus's followers refused to believe that He had been raised from the dead, but then as two of them were walking into the country, "he was revealed to them completely changed in appearance." "Then, after speaking to them, the Lord Jesus was taken up into heaven…"

In Luke, the men walking to Emmaus did not recognize Jesus even though he was walking alongside them, until they were given the key to this new format: when Jesus broke the bread and distributed it to them. Later, He let his Disciples touch him and he ate something to show them he wasn't a ghost. But then he blessed them and "was taken up to [a different format:] heaven."

And finally in John, Jesus tells Mary Magdalene "Do not cling to me for I have not yet ascended to the Father." And later: Even though the doors were locked, Jesus "came and stood before them."

There are other quotes in Scripture:

Jesus says: "Eye hath not seen…

"Where I am going, you cannot come…"

Yet: "He who sees me SEES the Father," as Roger Osgood has been emphasizing this summer.

Doesn't this all speak to a different format? Jesus seems to be saying: Don't look for me here, in your usual way: "Why are you standing looking up into heaven?" (ACTS). We have to be looking through different eyes, seeing reality in a different way, in a different format. That's called "being saved!" Because my wife couldn't find her book between two covers or in disc format didn't mean that it didn't exist! It just wasn't visible, touchable, enjoyable in those formats!

The Benedictine preacher, Fr. Laurence Freeman, writes:

The new kind of life made possible by the Resurrection does not rely upon the forensic evidence of the empty tomb or the circumstantial evidence of the apparitions. The evidence is found in daily living… It is the present moment illuminated with faith's ability to see the invisible, to recognize the obvious.[6]

In other words, Jesus asks all of us: "Who do you say I am?" And the answer is wherever we see him. "It is a field of consciousness similar to and indivisible from the Consciousness that is the God of cosmic and biblical revelation alike: the one great I AM." (Fr. Laurence).

So what could we do? How on earth does this help anything? Well, it could (COULD) help us understand where our dead loved ones are (how close they are) and it may even help us let go when it is our turn. But for now:

Think of it as a rediscovery. It's a resting in God as the logos, the explanation. We do not need some elaborate and confusing change-of-

6   Laurence Freeman OSB, "Letter Four," *The Web of Silence*. (New York: Continuum, 1998), 42-43.

format app. We are already in the format, but we may not be aware that we are. How do we access the Resurrection? That's easy. Jesus showed us. We do it through the cross; that is, through suffering, loss, through getting old, through dying, giving, loving, caring, seeking justice; and we practice it through meditation—through giving up the important things we have to do and say, and the important thoughts and plans we have to think and make, and just sitting, perhaps repeating our mantra, blank, open towards God, perhaps counting backwards from ten.

We have these giant weeds in the back of our house in Pennsylvania, and there's this one branch near the ground that—even on the quietist day when there seems to be no wind at all, this branch waves and dips and reminds us that we live in an atmosphere, in a soup we call air and which is continually moving, swirling, changing. And God? Well, writes Paul: "In him we live and move and have our Being." [Can we say: In His wind, we wave?]. To become aware of that is to find what we are looking for; and then finding that, it changes us profoundly.

Yep (to change the metaphor to John's): Even in darkness, the light shines, and the darkness cannot overcome it.   Amen.